Delaplaine's

2013 GUIDE TO SAN FRANCISCO

Last Update: 8 August 2013

Andrew Delaplaine

Copyright © 2013 by Gramercy Park Press
All rights reserved.
ISBN 978-1480157361

Please submit corrections, additions or comments to
andrewdelaplaine@mac.com

TABLES OF CONTENTS

Chapter 1 – FIRST THINGS FIRST
Why San Francisco? - 4
Transportation & Tips for Getting Around - 5
Specific Information During Your Visit - 6
Visitors' Centers - 6

Chapter 2 – LODGING
Downtown – 7
Fisherman's Wharf - 10
Union Square – SoMa - 13
The Castro – 18
Airport - 18
Nob Hill - 19

Chapter 3 – RESTAURANTS
Chinatown - 22
Embarcadero / Financial District - 23
Downtown / Union Square - 26
The Castro - 31
Haight-Ashbury - 32
Fisherman's Wharf - 33
The Mission - 35
Nob Hill - 37
Russian Hill - 39
Civic Center - 40
Pacific Heights - 41
SoMa - 41
Marina - 43
North Beach - 44
Sunset - 45

Chapter 4 – NIGHTLIFE
North Beach - 48
Financial District - 48
Haight-Ashbury - 49
The Mission - 50

SoMa - 52
Union Square – 54

SAN FRANCISCO GAY BARS
The Castro – 56
Lower Haight / Hayes Valley
SoMa (South of Market) - 60
Polk Street - 62
The Mission - 63

Chapter 5 – ATTRACTIONS - 66

Chapter 6 – SHOPPING
Chestnut Street - 77
Chinatown - 78
Embarcadero - 79
Fillmore Street - 81
Haight Street - 82
Hayes Valley - 83
North Beach - 84
The Mission - 84
Polk Street - 85
Sacramento Street - 86
Union Square - 87
Westfield - 87

Chapter 7 – THE WINE COUNTRY
Lodgings - 89
Restaurants - 95
Cooking Classes - 100
Attractions / Tours - 101
Spas - 106

INDEX – 108
RESTAURANTS BY CUISINE – 117
OTHER BOOKS BY THE SAME AUTHOR - 121

Chapter 1
FIRST THINGS FIRST

WHY SAN FRANCISCO?

The answer to this is quite simple: It truly is a beautiful city with great weather. Sure, the fog rolls into the bay quite often, but this only adds to the romance. No matter what neighborhood you find yourself in, it will be either very colorful or have outstanding views of the bay, Alcatraz, the Golden Gate Bridge. This combined with the genuine friendliness of San Franciscans will, as Tony Bennett sang, make you leave your heart here.

If you find yourself with nothing to do in the city, which is highly doubtful, there is always beach, mountains or forests just outside the city. Not too shabby.

There are only a handful of cities in the U.S. that I'd call completely unique: San Francisco is one of them. The "City by the Bay" has an allure like no other in the world. It has a dramatic setting that rivets the eye. No matter where you turn, there are spectacular vistas. Every neighborhood and even every street has a certain interesting "look" that's hard to describe.

The neighborhoods of San Francisco are entirely distinct. When you move from one area to another – from the Mission to Union Square to Pacific Heights to Fisherman's Wharf to Chinatown – you will find yourself in an entirely different environment, as if you'd traveled hundreds of miles. This is one thing that makes San Francisco so exciting: the huge range of diversity among its population.

The historical reputation of the city as a wild "anything goes" town from the Gold Rush Era has only slightly dissipated. The enormous gay population that gave modern San Francisco much of its outlaw glamour, devastated by the AIDS epidemic, still dominates large parts of the town. And while it looked like the bloom was off the rose for a few years, the city still has a dynamic and involved gay population.

It's nice to be able to take advantage of all the outdoor activities available here. I'm not out there doing these things, but YOU ought to be: go to Alcatraz, visit Golden Gate Park (and do NOT rush) because this is a place that has that San Francisco feel all over it, take the Coastal Trail, starting from the Cliff House, visit the Wine Country, take the Powell-Hyde cable car (these are not called "trolleys," but cable cars), walk (or bicycle) across the Golden Gate Bridge, walk along the Golden Gate Promenade, walk through the Haight to see what aging hippies really look like, walk up (or down) the Filbert Street Steps—these 380 steps lead you through some of the most interesting parts of town. You'll marvel at the varied architecture.

Other "musts" include a drink at the top of the Mark Hopkins, the St. Francis Drake or the Grand Hyatt. You won't soon forget the views.

They say that walking across the Golden Gate Bridge is one of those things you have to do once in your life. (I've never done that—I've always driven.) But that sentiment can be applied to the idea of just going to San Francisco itself. This visit *is* one of those things you have to do once in your life. And, if you're really a traveler, there's no way you'll not return.

TRANSPORTATION AND TIPS FOR GETTING AROUND

The fastest and cheapest way to get into the city from San Francisco International airport is by BART, the bay area's subway system. The route will take you about 35 minutes (depending on where you're going) and a one-way ticket will cost approximately $6. Trains depart every 15 minutes. If you want to take a cab, from the airport to downtown, it will cost you approximately $35-$40 plus tip and takes about 30 minutes, depending on traffic. Finally, you also have the Supershuttle option (800-258-3826). This is a private shuttle company that offers door-to-door service in which you share a van with a few other passengers. From the airport it will be $15 per person to a residence or business. On the return trip to the airport, add $8-$15 for each additional person depending on whether they pick you up from a business or residence.

Taxis from Oakland International Airport are pricey, about $50 plus tip. Then you have the Bayporter Express (877-467-1800), a shuttle service that costs $26 for the first person and $12 for each additional person in your party. Children 11 and under pay $7 and they do accept advance reservations. There are also other shuttles that will charge you about $20 to take you into the city but these are independently owned and costs will vary. Again, the cheapest way into the city from this airport is by BART. Here though you will need to board the AirBART shuttle to the terminals that the actual train to the city departs from. The entire cost will be approximately $5.50 and the entire excursion will take around 45 minutes.

Aside from the obvious options of having a car or using a cab, once you're in the city, their public transportation will make it very easy for you to get around. Not only can you take the subway, BART just about anywhere, they also have two separate bus systems you can take SamTrans and MUNI. You will find all of these three options very convenient.

SPECIFIC INFORMATION DURING YOUR VISIT

sfweekly.com
This will give you specific information on events, galleries and goings-on around the city the week you are actually there.

baycitizen.org
Another weekly paper filled with local news, events and information during your visit.

sanfrancisco.travel
Specific information for visitors.

VISITORS' CENTERS

The California Welcome Center San Francisco
Pier 39
Building B, Level 2
San Francisco, CA 94133-1006
visitcwc.com/SanFrancisco

Napa Valley Welcome Center
600 Main Street
Napa, CA 94559
Phone: 707-251-5895

Lodging assistance: 707-251-9188
http://www.visitnapavalley.com

Sonoma Valley Vintners & Growers
783 Broadway
Sonoma, CA 95476
Phone: 707-935-0803
Fax: 707-935-1947
Email: info@sonomavalleywine.com
sonomavalleywine.com

Chapter 2
LODGING

DOWNTOWN LODGING
The area is marked by the cluster of high-rise towers that lies between Grant Avenue east of the Union Square shopping district, Sacramento Street and Columbus Street, south of Chinatown and North Beach, and the Embarcadero that rings the waterfront.

THE ARCHBISHOP'S MANSION
1000 Fulton St., San Francisco: 415-563-7872
NO WEBSITE
Built in 1904 for Archbishop Patrick Riordan. Rooms are individually decorated. Beyond the antique furnishings, a massive redwood fireplace with Corinthian columns dominates the front parlor. From the foyer, a three-story staircase (sweeping majestically up to the guest rooms and suites) is illuminated by a 16-foot-wide stained-glass dome that miraculously survived the 1906 earthquake. All the rooms have queen-size or larger beds, 19th-century French antiques, fine linens and silks and private baths. Many feature fireplaces.

BAY BRIDGE INN
966 Harrison St., San Francisco: 415-397-0657
baybridgeinn.com
Located in the heart of San Francisco, the Bay Bridge Inn is within walking distance of the Pacific Bell Park which is the home of the San Francisco Giants, the Moscone Convention Center and the Museum of Modern Art.

COURTYARD BY MARRIOTT SAN FRANCISCO DOWNTOWN
299 Second St., San Francisco: 415-947-0700
marriott.com
Courtyard Downtown San Francisco Hotel by Marriott, an urban Courtyard located just blocks from MOMA, the Moscone Center and the Embarcadero. The hotel offers the amenities of a luxury hotel such as valet parking, a Starbucks and Whispers Bar and Grill in the lobby, Jasmines Restaurant for breakfast, room service, event catering, indoor pool, and complete fitness room at a price that other luxury hotels cannot touch.

DAKOTA HOTEL AND HOSTEL
606 Post St., San Francisco: 415-931-7475
dakotahostelsanfrancisco.com
Located right next to Union Station, the cable cars, department stores, the financial district and convention centers, this hotel is in an ideal location for tourists, business travelers and conventioneers. The Dakota also has a separate section that caters to backpackers.

DAYS INN
895 Geary St., San Francisco: 415-441-8220
daysinn.com
The Days Inn is located in the Downtown San Francisco area. Located in the middle of the Theatre District. You have found the perfect location in the heart of San Francisco. Large, beautifully decorated guest rooms, electronic keys, and interior halls. Control your own air conditioning and heat. Each room features a hair dryer, iron and ironing board, color TV with cable, AM/FM Clock Radio, private bath with tub, shower, and dressing area.

DAYS INN AT THE BEACH
2600 Sloat Blvd., San Francisco: 415-665-5440
daysinn.com
Located 4 miles from San Francisco downtown and 12 miles from San Francisco Airport, in a quiet neighborhood across from the San Francisco Zoo, just a short stroll to the beach. Close to the public transportation, VA Medical Center, Shriners Hospital and San Francisco State University.

KNIGHTS INN DOWNTOWN SAN FRANCISCO
240 7th St., San Francisco: 415-861-6469
knightsinn.com
This hotel is located in the downtown area and offers easy access to all major attractions. It's just 3 blocks from the convention center and cable car station. Hotel offers free limited parking ($24 value) and a Lite Continental Breakfast which includes choices of coffee, tea, juice and a pastry only each morning in the main lobby hospitality area from 6-9am ($7 value).

MANDARIN ORIENTAL
222 Sansome St., San Francisco: 415-276-9888
www.mandarinoriental.com
Rooms here are situated between floors 38 and 48 of this tower. Here you'll be more interested in the views from the rooms than the rooms themselves, even though the rooms are lavish, with marble baths and every amenity

you can think of. The high elevation gives you unparalleled views of the city. If you're lucky enough to see the fog creep in from the bay, you'll be rewarded with a memorable experience. If you're going to pay for a suite in San Francisco, you can't do better than to get one of these 2,000-square-foot gems. Nice tea service in lobby.

MARRIOTT SAN FRANCISCO
55 Fourth St., San Francisco 415-896-1600
marriott.com
Rising 39 stories high in the skyline, the magnificent Marriott Marquis San Francisco Hotel exudes an essence of modern luxury and the convenience of an extraordinary downtown San Francisco hotel. Just south of Market Street, this San Francisco, California hotel next to the Moscone Convention Center is steps away from the Yerba Buena Gardens, renowned museums and cultural attractions, world-class shopping on Union Square, and AT&T Park, home of the San Francisco Giants.

THE MOSSER HOTEL
54 Fourth St., San Francisco: 415-986-4400
themosser.com
Centrally located in the heart of downtown San Francisco, with a recent six million dollar renovation, this Union Square boutique hotel offers sleek design and fine-tuned guestrooms that fuse historical touches with streamlined sophistication. Opened in 1913 as the Keystone Hotel, this historic property has offered a delightful experience for Bay Area visitors for almost 100 years. In 1981, Charles W. Mosser purchased the hotel and after a multi-million dollar renovation in 2003, he renamed it The Mosser. Like San Francisco, The Mosser offers a unique, care free culture mixed with the splendor of yester-year. This is apparent in the fusion of Victorian architecture mixed with modern interior design.

OMNI SAN FRANCISCO HOTEL
500 California St., San Francisco: 415-677-9494
omnihotels.com/findahotel/sanfrancisco.aspx
The Omni Hotel provides instant access to the Financial District, walking distance to Union Square, Nob Hill & Embarcadero Center. Ideal for a romantic getaway, the Omni San Francisco Hotel offers modern amenities in a boutique ambiance due to its Florentine Renaissance architecture. Built as a bank in 1926, the lobby is adorned with Italian marble, rich fabrics and Austrian crystal chandeliers.

RENOIR HOTEL
45 McAllister St., San Francisco: 415-626-5200
renoirhotel.com
The Renoir Hotel is a cosmopolitan, European-style hotel in a 100 year old historical landmark building, conveniently located in the heart of downtown San Francisco on Market Street, between the Orpheum and the Golden Gate Theaters. Easy access to all public transportation including BART (airport connection), Muni subway, Streetcars for Fisherman's Wharf and the Castro, as well as buses to all parts of the city (incl. Golden Gate Transit to the Golden Gate Bridge and Sausalito).

WHARF LODGING
There's something for everyone at Fisherman's Wharf: food, views, history, family fun and more. A food lover's haven, Fisherman's Wharf boasts some of the best dining in the world. During the day, street performers are here to tirelessly entertain you: magicians, mimes, musicians, jugglers, clowns and fire-eaters take pride in their efforts to make you feel welcome at Fisherman's Wharf.

BAYSIDE INN AT THE WHARF
1201 Columbus Ave., San Francisco: 415-776-7070
baysideinnwharf.com
Bayside Inn at the Wharf is located in the heart of San Francisco's tourist district. This Fisherman's Wharf inn is walking distance from city and Alcatraz tours, Pier 39, restaurants, bars, North Beach Italian District, Ghirardelli Square, cable car pick-ups and the famous section of Lombard Street known as "Crookedest Street." Air-Conditioned. Free Newspaper. Cable TV. Coffee Maker. Data Line.

FAIRMONT HERITAGE PLACE GHIRARDELLI SQUARE
900 N. Point St., San Francisco: 415-268-9900
www.fairmontheritageplace.com/heritageplace/Ghirardelli
Airport transportation, concierge services and a fitness center. Set on the city's dynamic waterfront, Fairmont's sister hotel by the Bay offers the ideal base from which to explore the city. From arranging dinner reservations or sailing excursions to booking tickets for theatrical, cultural, or sporting events, their unparalleled personalized service allows you convenient access to all that San Francisco has to offer.

HILTON SAN FRANCISCO FISHERMAN'S WHARF
2620 Jones St., San Francisco: 415-885-4700

www.hilton.com
Opened in April 2000 and nestled in the world-famous Fisherman's Wharf district, this hotel got a $9 million transformation with attractive guest rooms and many guest amenities.

HOLIDAY INN EXPRESS & SUITES FISHERMAN'S WHARF
550 N. Point St., San Francisco: 415-409-4600
hiefishermanswharf.com
All rooms feature Broadband internet connection, free local calls and free express breakfast daily. When searching for San Francisco hotels near Fisherman's Wharf, this is a good bet. Positioned just steps from the top-visited attraction in the city, guests enjoy effortless access to most major businesses and the must-visit destinations in San Francisco.

HOLIDAY INN FISHERMAN'S WHARF
1300 Columbus Ave., San Francisco: 415-771-9000
hifishermanswharf.com
The Holiday Inn Fisherman's Wharf features room service, a pool area, airport transportation and a concierge. They are just a block from Fisherman's Wharf waterfront and minutes from the Financial District.

HYATT AT FISHERMAN'S WHARF
555 N. Point St., San Francisco: 415-563-1234
fishermanswharf.hyatt.com
Easy access to Pier 39, the Cannery, Harbor Cruises and Ghirardelli Square. The Hyatt provides medium-sized guest rooms with laundry facilities.

MARRIOTT AT FISHERMAN'S WHARF
1250 Columbus Ave., San Francisco: 415-775-7555
marriott.com
Standard issue Marriott.

RADISSON FISHERMAN'S WHARF
250 Beach St., San Francisco: 415-392-6700
radisson.com
The Radisson is the only bayfront hotel at Fisherman's Wharf. Close to Pier 39, Alcatraz Island, Ghirardelli Square and cable cars. Select rooms feature views of the bay, and all guests enjoy free high-speed, wireless Internet; outdoor swimming pool open all year, Fitness Center, Business Center, meeting services and concierge staff.

SAN REMO HOTEL
2237 Mason St., San Francisco: 415-776-8688
sanremohotel.com
The hotel ambiance is Old World: quiet rooms without phones or TVs, Victorian heirloom furnishings and hallways lined with historic photos. Guests share bath facilities, reminiscent of European pensione-style lodging. There are few concessions to modern times, but travelers will find dial-up and wireless Internet access in the main hallway. Alternative Lifestyle Friendly. Self Parking. Parking Fee.

SHERATON FISHERMAN'S WHARF
2500 Mason St., San Francisco: 415-362-5500
sheratonatthewharf.com
Renovated in 1995, the Sheraton is located in the heart of Fisherman's Wharf. Guest rooms feature in-room movies, voice mail and video check-out. Services include salon, gift shop and tour desk.

THE SUITES AT FISHERMAN'S WHARF
2655 Hyde St., San Francisco: 415-771-0200
thesuitesatfishermanswharf.com
Opened in 1986 and renovated in 1997, this all suite non-smoking hotel features fully stocked kitchens with cappuccino makers. Located near Ghirardelli Square, Hyde Street cable car turnaround, and restaurants.

UNION SQUARE/ SOMA LODGING

Union Square has also come to describe not just the plaza itself, but the general shopping, dining, and theater districts within the surrounding blocks. The Geary and Curran theaters one block west on Geary anchor the "theater district" and border the Tenderloin. Union Square is also home to San Francisco's TIX Bay Area, a half-priced ticket booth and Ticketmaster outlet. Run by Theatre Bay Area, tickets for most of San Francisco's performing arts can be purchased the day of the performance at a discounted rate.

ADAGIO
550 Geary St., San Francisco: 415-775-5000
www.thehoteladagio.com
If you're looking for a moderately priced hotel in the Union Square area, this is a great choice. The Spanish-style structure is from 1929 and has a great feel to it. It's not a small property (some 170 rooms), but there's a wide range of choice among the lodgings here. There are 2 suites in the

penthouse (go for the one with the terrace). There's also an "executive" section from the 7th to the 16th floors that have additional amenities.

CLIFT
495 Geary St. (at Taylor), San Francisco: 800-697-1791
www.clifthotel.com
This used to be one of my favorite old hotels in San Francisco until Ian Schrager came in and did his usual number on the place. Now, with its Philippe Starck designed rooms and lobby, it's become one in a long line of trendy hotels owned by Schrager. Sometimes, what he does is great (the Delano in South Beach, the Royalton in New York), but other times he misses the mark (the Gramercy Park in New York being an example—I am *not* a fan of the Julian Schnabel interiors). What's fun about the place is to bounce in here and mix and mingle with the trendy crowd, if that's your thing and you don't mind the snooty staff. But avoid the restaurant here, **Asia de Cuba**. But *do* check out the **Redwood Room**. It's a winner.

FOUR SEASONS
757 Market St., San Francisco: 415-633-3000
www.fourseasons.com
The hushed elegance of this fine hotel almost puts you on your guard when you walk into the lobby from the elevators. It's almost as if you don't want to be caught speaking in a loud voice. But this is no library, Mary. It's just a wonderfully understated luxury property staffed with some of the best professionals in the business. Coming from South Beach as I do, I'm a big fan of fine hotels with superior staff, something South Beach is not known for. (The staff always *look* good, but that's usually as far as it goes.) San Francisco is one of those cities where you have to fight yourself to choose which one you'll experience on this trip. Can't go wrong here.

GOLDEN GATE HOTEL
775 Bush St., San Francisco: 415-392-3702
www.goldengatehotel.com
Another nicely priced alternative, just a couple of blocks from Union Square and also two blocks from Nob Hill. You'll fall in love with this family run property in a 1913 building with a very distinctive feel to it. If you come back here often, you'll note that no room is decorated like any of the others. Antiques, nice quilted bedspreads, other pleasant touches. Only 25 rooms. (About half have private baths, the others share.) Free afternoon tea and Continental breakfast. They have a deal with a health club a block away that you can use.

GRAND HYATT
345 Stockton St., San Francisco: 415-398-1234
grand.hyatt.com
Another example of a truly regal hotel in a city noted for them. Big pluses: right in the heart of the best shopping district; stunning views from almost all the rooms; recently renovated and upgrades rooms and amenities; a lobby that makes you feel special just by walking into it (note the huge vases and Chinese décor); a section of rooms (23 of them) specially decontaminated so they're free of viruses and bacteria.
If you stay in the **Regency Club** rooms for an extra $50, you get a special lounge, free bar, free Continental breakfast and a spread of canapés at cocktail hour. (Well worth the $50, right?) They also have a deal that offers business people a room with a copier, printer, office supplies and other benefits. Ask about it.

GRIFFON
155 Steuart St. (bet. Mission & Howard), San Francisco: 415-495-2100
www.hotelgriffon.com
With only 62 very prime units, the Griffon is one of the better small properties in town. Lots of amenities, nice high ceilings. Renovated just a few years ago, beautifully maintained. It's by the waterfront and very close to the Financial District. Attracts discriminating travelers. Try to get one of the rooms overlooking the Bay Bridge. No smoking anywhere on property.

HARBOR COURT
165 Steuart St. (bet. Mission & Howard), San Francisco: 415-882-1300
www.harborcourthotel.com
It costs a bit more to stay in a room with views of the bay, but go the extra mile, because it's really worth it. This nice property near the Financial District that you don't hear that much about, but it's *always* bustling with an interesting mix of people. Just off the Embarcadero. Gets a lot of upper end business types. But these mix well at the jam packed happy hours in the **Ozumo Sushi Bar** that attracts a lot of other types to the place. Another plus is the access you get to the YMCA next door with its fully equipped club and indoor pool. Oh, and there's a wine tasting every evening that's a nice touch.

THE PALACE
2 New Montgomery St. (at Market St.), San Francisco: 415-512-1111
www.sfpalace.com
The original building dates from 1875 and when it was built, it was one of the biggest and grandest hotels in the world. It had to be restored after the

devastating earthquake of 1906. And while the rooms are nice in an old fashioned way, what you come here for is merely to walk through the doors into the lobby, especially into the **Garden Court**, one of the most stunning rooms of its kind. (It makes the Palm Court at New York's Plaza look like a corner teashop by comparison.) There are some 80,000+ pieces of glass in the ceiling here. It's worth a visit just to see this room and its elaborate chandeliers. Do your best to have high tea here. Another eatery in the Palace is **The Pied Piper Bar & Grill**, a typical grand hotel grill that's very good.,

PALOMAR
12 Fourth St (at Market St.), San Francisco: 415-348-1111
www.hotelpalomar-sf.com
A very different sort of San Francisco experience. This hotel is situated on the top 5 floors of an office building that went up in 1907. (There's a special private entrance through the back for VIPs.) Very elegant rooms. Understated Art Deco interiors. Perfect for a secret liaison. Don't overlook the restaurant here, the **Fifth Floor**. Expensive but it's one of the best in town.

REX
562 Sutter St., San Francisco: 415-433-4434
thehotelrex.com
The hotel near Union Square used to be a bookstore before being converted into a hotel in the late '90s. There's even a sign that announces: "Book Nerds Welcome." As an homage to its previous life, they have literary events throughout the year. Vintage typewriters and books are everywhere in the lobby and the Library Bar (you'll love this bar with its soft cushy chairs and dark paneling and wooden columns). Ask about the "Tour de Rex," which is a tour they've developed that highlights important literary spots throughout the city. (They give you a Globe bike and a special map.) Moderate rates.

SIR FRANCIS DRAKE
450 Powell St. (at Sutter St.), San Francisco: 800-795-7129
www.sirfrancisdrake.com
Right in the middle of Union Square you'll find this stately property. It's part of the Kimpton chain, and they've spared no expense keeping this 1928 gem in tip-top shape. There's always something going on here. You've got **Scala's Bistro** on the ground floor that's a lively and bustling place (the Mediterranean food is excellent), there's **Caffe Espresso** makes a great place to stop for a coffee and pastry, but their selection of sandwiches is

also wide-ranging. Finally, there's **Harry Denton's Starlight Room** way up top where you'd be crazy not to go to take in the view.

ST. REGIS
125 Third St., San Francisco: 415-284-4000
www.stregis.com
Only open since 2005, this stunning addition to the local hotel scene has muscled aside some older pretenders to attract not only a trendy crowd, but as lot of the city's older social element as well. Nice touches like the 15-foot long fireplace in the bar attract your attention. They have a personal butler to take you to your room to show you a remote device that controls everything in the room. Home to **Remede Spa**, a two-floor oasis you'll love.

STRATFORD HOTEL
242 Powell St., San Francisco: 415-397-7080
hotelstratford.com
Built in 1907 and renovated in 1997, the Stratford is a European hotel and provides guests with free access to a large indoor heated pool and exercise facility at their sister hotel. Free continental breakfast included.

UNION SQUARE
114 Powell St., San Francisco: 415-397-3000
www.hotelunionsquare.com
Nice moderately priced alternative with distinctive décor. Can't beat the location.

VITALE
8 Mission St. (at Embarcadero), San Francisco: 415-413-4716
http://jdvhotels25-px.trvlclick.com/hotels/sanfrancisco/vitale
Here with a waterfront location is a great hotel (with a nice spa), close to the Ferry Building at the foot of Market Street. Be sure to look into the Railway Museum located inside the hotel.

W SAN FRANCISCO
181 Third St. (bet. Mission & Howard), San Francisco: 415-777-5300
www.whotels.com
Cool, cool, cool. What else can one say about the W, whether it's here or in South Beach? That little sign at the concierge desk? "Whatever. Whenever." All right, it may be a trifle on the specious side, but they seem to pull it off, as long as you don't mind the relentless posturing. Ultra hip and modern rooms with great color schemes. (The rooms have names like "Cool Corner" or "Extreme Wow Suite.") Rooms also have little touches you

won't expect: a Buddha figurine, other knick-knacks. Bliss products are in the rooms, and part of the hotel is the **Bliss Spa**, a branch of the one in New York. (This one is 5,000 square feet.) Nightlife lovers flock here because so much nightlife takes place inside the hotel itself. **The Living Room Bar** is an intoxicating space filled with vibrant lights, tunes and hues.

WESTIN ST. FRANCIS
335 Powell St., San Francisco: 415-397-7000
westin.com/stfrancis
This is one of those hotels you just have to visit, even if you're not staying there. Go in for a drink if nothing else. Overlooking Union Square in downtown San Francisco, the 1904 landmark St. Francis Hotel offers luxurious guest rooms, world-class dining and meeting facilities. More than just a hotel, The Westin St. Francis is a destination where you can unwind and be pampered by attentive, world-class service.

WARWICK REGIS HOTEL
490 Geary St. at Taylor, San Francisco: 415-928-7900
warwicksf.com
The Warwick Regis Hotel features room service, a pool area. Warwick Regis Hotel is a 3 star hotel with a setting where you can have a real Boutique / Design Hotels experience. 1 km from San Francisco city center.

THE CASTRO LODGING
The Castro is one of America's first and best-known gay neighborhoods, and it is currently the largest. Having transformed from a working-class neighborhood through the 1960s and 1970s, the Castro remains a symbol and source of lesbian, gay, bisexual, and transgender (LGBT) activism and events.

BECK'S MOTOR LODGE
2222 Market St., San Francisco: 415-621-8212
becksmotorlodge.com
The colorful Castro District in San Francisco is home to this charming lodge, nestled on a tree-lined street near local attractions and offering comfortable accommodations and thoughtful amenities. Air-Conditioned. Cable TV. Coffee Maker. Hair Dryer. Fireplace. Data Line. Voice Mail. Wi-Fi.

AIRPORT LODGING

San Francisco International Airport SFO is one of the country's busiest airports and is gateway to the Pacific regions. SFO serves the cosmopolitan city of San Francisco, Silicon Valley, and the wider Bay Area. The Airport is located next to the cities of Millbrae & San Bruno, in San Mateo County, 13 miles south of San Francisco.

HOWARD JOHNSON HOTEL & SUITES
222 S. Airport Blvd., South San Francisco: 650-589-9055
hojosfo.com
Located just a mile away from the airport, the Howard Johnson Hotel & Suites is just a short distance away from several fine attractions. A restaurant and lounge are located next door. Airport transportation.

HYATT REGENCY SAN FRANCISCO AIRPORT
1333 Bayshore Hwy., Burlingame: 650-347-1234
sanfranciscoairport.hyatt.com
The Hyatt Regency San Francisco Airport features room service, a pool area, 50,880 square feet of meeting space and airport transportation.

LA QUINTA INN SOUTH
20 Airport Blvd. S., South San Francisco: 650-583-2223
lq.com
The La Quinta Inn South features a pool area and an exercise room. Free Breakfast.

MARRIOTT SAN FRANCISCO AIRPORT
1800 Old Bayshore Hwy., Burlingame: 650-692-9100
marriott.com
24 hour free airport shuttle is available to hotel guests. The San Francisco Airport Marriott hotel in Burlingame, CA is just minutes from the San Francisco International Airport and 15 miles from downtown San Francisco, offering a great location with great views of the San Francisco Bay to all types of travelers.

NOB HILL LODGING

The area was settled in the rapid urbanization happening in the city in the late 19th century. Because of the views and its central position, it became an exclusive enclave of the rich and famous on the west coast who built large mansions in the neighborhood. This included prominent tycoons such as Leland Stanford, founder of Stanford University, and other members of The Big Four.

BOHEME
444 Columbus Ave., San Francisco: 415-433-9111
www.hotelboheme.com
This could as easily be placed in the North Beach section, because it's right there: all the shops, restaurants and bars dotting Columbus Avenue. This is the perfect kind of place to stay in because it's easy to walk to Union Square and Chinatown. The Boheme is just the opposite of the ultra-luxury hotels in this town. Quaint rooms, beautifully decorated, very homey. There's not even a lobby (although in the small lobby they do serve sherry in the afternoons), just a small area big enough for Reception. Rooms on the street are pretty noisy. Still, a wonderful property.

THE FAIRMONT
950 Mason St., San Francisco: 415-772-5000
fairmont.com/sanfrancisco
Built in 1906, this distinguished and historic hotel atop Nob Hill has convenient access to the cable car line. The Tower's modern guest rooms feature panoramic views of the bay and city. The main building has a Victorian decor. Large gift shop and store.

THE HUNTINGTON
1075 California St. (bet. Mason & Taylor), San Francisco: 800-227-4683
www.huntingtonhotel.com
This is a unique property among the top tier lavish hotels in San Francisco because it's still family-owned, not part of some multinational conglomerate. Everything is done with extreme good taste here at the Huntington. The rooms are enormous and look to me like they've all been decorated individually. Lots of antiques, excellent quality linens. The restaurant here, **Big Four**, is fun because it's so old fashioned. (The menu offers high quality American cuisine.) It's also quite well known as a spa destination because its **Nob Hill Spa** is considered one of the best in town.

INTERCONTINENTAL MARK HOPKINS
1 Nob Hill (bet. California & Mason Sts.), San Francisco: 800-972-3124
www.intercontinental.com
Some would call this the grandest dame of all the other *grand dame* hotels in San Francisco, but if you spend enough time visiting, you'll soon find the one you like the best. The rooms (and especially the HUGE suites) are lavish to the point that they look like movie sets. All the best amenities. (It costs over $50 to valet your car!) The most famous thing about this hotel has got to the **Top of the Mark**, and it's as captivating on the fiftieth visit as

it is the first time you ever walk into the place and take a look at that view. They have a Sunday brunch that's a real treat, but it's at night that the place really shines.

NOB HILL MOTOR INN
1630 Pacific Ave., San Francisco: 415-775-8160
nobhillmotorinn.com
The Nob Hill Motor Inn is located in the Pacific Heights/Russian Hill area and within walking distance to many restaurants, shops, Fisherman's Wharf, Chinatown, cable cars, North Beach, the Opera House and many other major attractions. Parking is free.

THE RITZ-CARLTON
600 Stockton St. (bet. Pine and California), San Francisco: 415-296-7465
ritzcarlton.com
This nine-story exclusive hotel is set on top Nob Hill's eastern slope and is on the California St. Cable Car line. The landmark building borders the city's Financial District, Chinatown and Union Street. This property was renovated in 2006, though it was nearly perfect beforehand. The building in which this luxury hotel is housed was once the Metropolitan Insurance Company. The Ritz people bought it, gutted it and transformed it into one of the finest hotels in the country. Afternoon tea and Sunday brunch are real treats here.

STANFORD COURT
905 California St. (at Powell), San Francisco: 415-989-3500
www.stanfordcourt.com
While you feel like you're going back in time to the 19th century when you walk into this lavish lobby with its dome of stained glass, its Baccarat chandeliers and its museum-quality selection of European antiques, it's really a very modern hotel operated with the serenity and panache of a Continental throwback. Although they charge you an arm and a leg, they don't charge you for coffee or tea in your room in the morning, one among many other nice touches that will endear you to this wonderful hotel. (It's named after Leland Stanford, whose house used to stand on this site in much the same was as railroad king Mark Hopkins's house stood at the hotel that bears his name.)

Chapter 3
RESTAURANTS

WINE GUIDE
It never hurts to keep current on the latest vintages, so I always recommend you get the new edition of <u>Hugh Johnson's Pocket Wine Book 2013</u>. It runs to some 300 pages. (You can get the ebook at online retailers for about $10, or a used hardcover copy for about $7 + shipping, depending on your preference. Hugh Johnson is a towering figure among wine writers. (I always trust him more than I do Parker, who's a bit of a pompous blowhard.)

CHINATOWN
San Francisco Chinatown is the largest Chinatown outside of Asia as well as the oldest Chinatown in North America. It is one of the top tourist attractions in San Francisco. The reality of Chinatown is that there are two Chinatowns: One belongs to the locals, the other charms the tourists. They overlap and dance with each other, drawing more visitors annually than the Golden Gate Bridge.

Since its establishment in 1848, it has been highly important and influential in the history and culture of ethnic Chinese immigrants to the United States and North America. Chinatown is an active enclave that continues to retain its own customs, languages, places of worship, social clubs, and identity.

EMPRESS OF CHINA
838 Grant Ave., San Francisco: 415-434-1345
empressofchinasf.com
CUISINE: Chinese
DRINKS: Full Bar
SERVING: Lunch/ Dinner

The quality of decor at this Chinatown institution surpasses the quality of its food. Filled with temple artifacts and grand chandeliers, Empress exudes an air of elegance. The restaurant's sixth-floor views over Portsmouth Square are worth a look, but its basic Cantonese cuisine pales in comparison.

HANG AH TEA ROOM
1 Pagoda Pl., San Francisco: 415-982-5686
NO WEBSITE
CUISINE: Chinese
DRINKS: Beer/ Wine
SERVING: Lunch/ Dinner
Tucked away in one of Chinatown's small alleys, bills itself as San Francisco's oldest dim sum house. Opened in 1920, the colorful decor in this tiny spot reflects the equally colorful fare. Popular edibles include barbecue pork steam buns, shrimp dumplings, and sticky rice with pork. For dessert Hang Ah serves homemade ice cream in fruity flavors, such as fresh mango. The restaurant also serves pearl drinks, made from tapioca and various fruits.

JAI YUN
680 Clay St., San Francisco: 415-981-7438
CUISINE: Chinese
DRINKS: Beer/ Wine
SERVING: Dinner
No website
Hailing from Nanjing, a couple of hundred miles from Shanghai, Chef Ji Nei' focuses on light and delicate flavors, often steaming or brining the food. He is said to shop every day in Chinatown, which means the menu changes nightly depending on his finds. Foo yung abalone (scrambled eggs with shellfish) is one specialty. He's also known for his quail soup and basil-mushroom stirfry.

R&G LOUNGE
631 Kearny St., San Francisco: 415-982-7877
rnglounge.com
CUISINE: Chinese
DRINKS: Full Bar
SERVING: Lunch/ Dinner
Chinese businessmen frequent the upstairs area at R&G Lounge, where Cantonese banquet menus are the usual, featuring fresh produce and fresh

fish. The downstairs gets packed at lunchtime with locals gorging on the cheap rice plates.

YUET LEE SEAFOOD RESTAURANT
1300 Stockton St., San Francisco: 415-982-6020
NO WEBSITE
CUISINE: Chinese
DRINKS: Beer/ Wine
SERVING: Lunch/ Dinner
If you simply must have frog legs at two in the morning, this is the place. The atmosphere in the after-drinking hours is jovial, and the lazy Susan overflows with spicy condiments.

EMBARCADERO/FINANCIAL DISTRICT
Embarcadero Station is a Muni Metro and Bay Area Rapid Transit station near the Embarcadero in the Financial District of San Francisco, California. It is located at the north-eastern end of the Market Street Subway below Market Street between Spear Street and Beale Street.

750 RESTAURANT & BAR
750 Kearny St., San Francisco: 415-433-6600
sf-restaurant.asp
CUISINE: American/ Asian
DRINKS: Full Bar
SERVING: Breakfast/Lunch/Dinner
Located at the crossroads of Chinatown, North Beach and the Financial District, 750 Restaurant & Bar is the perfect location for a healthy meal. With choices as diverse as the neighborhood, enjoy a savory blend of East Meets West with a Northern California twist. Signature dishes include Seared Ahi Won Tons, Grilled Berkshire Pork Chop and Soy Lacquered Short Ribs.

ALFRED'S STEAKHOUSE
659 Merchant St., San Francisco: 415-781-7058
alfredssteakhouse.com
CUISINE: Steakhouse
DRINKS: Full Bar
SERVING: Dinner
Alfred's Steakhouse, since 1928, is a classic steakhouse serving massive cuts of beef in a plush dining room. If it's steak you want, this is the place to

be. Extensive whiskey and single malt scotch selections. Outstanding martinis. Four rooms for private dining.

BIX
56 Gold St., San Francisco: 415-433-6300
bixrestaurant.com
CUISINE: American/ Californian
DRINKS: Full bar
SERVING: Dinner
An exceptionally stylish supper club, civilized speakeasy, a sophisticated saloon. Each of these "personae" is housed in a soaring two-story interior distinguished by a gently curving mahogany bar, fluted columns with ornate capitals, stunning original art, plush banquettes, cozy booths, starched linens, glittering glasses, and polished flatware. Overall, the ambiance is tasteful Art Moderne reminiscent of the glory days of Cunard and French Line ships. Fashionable and glamorous are the hallmarks. Trendy is simply not a part of the BIX culture. The clientele at BIX ranges from San Francisco movers-and-shakers to "savvy travelers" - owner Doug Biederbeck's term for the many diners in the know from out of town who patronize his establishment. All of them step from the featureless alley into another world, a world of superb cookery and libations, of sparkling service, of stylish nostalgia, of polished live jazz.

COTOGNA
490 Pacific Ave., San Francisco: 415-775-8508
cotognasf.com
CUISINE: Italian/ Pizza
DRINKS: Full Bar
SERVING: Lunch/Dinner
Located in the heart of San Francisco's historic Jackson Square neighborhood, Cotogna is a lively, comfortably-stylish restaurant featuring rustic Italian trattoria cuisine. Seasonally-changing menu features spit-roasted or grilled meats and game birds, wood-oven pizzas, house-made pastas, fresh local fish and seafood, salads, salumi and cheeses in the warm atmosphere of the restaurant's refined urban design.

HECHO
185 Sutter St., San Francisco: 415-835-6400
hechosf.com
CUISINE: Japanese/ Sushi
DRINKS: Full Bar
SERVING: Breakfast/Lunch/Dinner

After extensive travels to Mexico to study tequila, Mexican food and culture, coupled with extensive travels to Japan to study Japanese food, culture, restaurant architecture and design, Joseph Manzare created Hecho. High end Japanese sushi and robata. The bar features over 80 premium brand tequilas, plus an extensive sake program. The name Hecho comes from the Spanish word for "made."

PALIO D'ASTI
640 Sacramento St., San Francisco: 415-395-9800
paliodasti.com
CUISINE: Italian
DRINKS: Full Bar
SERVING: Lunch/Dinner
The award winning, 7,000 square foot restaurant interior is so designed as to permit the viewing of the chefs as they prepare Italian dishes with particular emphasis on the regions of Piemonte and Toscana.

PERRY'S
155 Steuart St., San Francisco: 415-495-6500
Original location at 1944 Union St., 415-922-9022
perryssf.com
CUISINE: American
DRINKS: Full Bar
SERVING: Breakfast/Lunch/Dinner
Perry's on the Embarcadero is the newest outpost of the Union Street original, now in its 40th year. Perry's has become a San Francisco institution, known for its classic American food, its warm personable service and a fun, bustling bar. Opens for breakfast early and the bar is open late, serving drinks and snacks until midnight Thursday through Saturday. Perry's signature dishes include French onion soup, traditional Cobb salad, petrale sole meuniere, a selection of prime steaks and of course, the renowned hamburger that made it famous.

DOWNTOWN/ UNION SQUARE
Union Square is a plaza bordered by Geary, Powell, Post and Stockton Streets in San Francisco, California. "Union Square" also refers to the central shopping, hotel, and theater district that surrounds the plaza for several blocks.

AKIKO'S RESTAURANT & SUSHI BAR
431 Bush St., San Francisco: 415-397-3218

akikosrestaurant.com
CUISINE: Japanese/ Sushi
DRINKS: Beer
SERVING: Lunch/Dinner
The quality of the sushi is attributed to a one-of-a-kind combination of fresh ingredients, coupled with 26 years of experience and unique preparation techniques. "Akiko" means "autumn child; iris, bright and light" in Japanese.

AMBER INDIA
25 Yerba Buena Ln., San Francisco: 415- 777-0500
www.amber-india.com/
CUISINE: Indian
DRINKS: Full bar
SERVING: Lunch/Dinner
Embodies the spirit and essence of fine Indian cuisine. Located in the heart of downtown San Francisco, Amber India Restaurant takes Indian cuisine to a new culinary level, while still holding true to its traditional nuances. Much like the ambiance within the restaurant, Amber India's cuisine is a mix of modern style with traditional roots. The delectable cuisine, the well paired wines, and the exotic cocktails are sure to indulge anyone's senses.

ANZU
222 Mason St., San Francisco: 415- 394-1100
restaurantanzu.com
CUISINE: Californian/ Steakhouse/ Sushi
DRINKS: Full bar
SERVING: Breakfast/Lunch/Dinner
The elegant and intimate Restaurant ANZU, located on the second level of Hotel Nikko, is one of San Francisco's most acclaimed dining experiences. Here, sustainable California cuisine is enhanced with Asian flavors, creating a whole new delicious gourmet culture that patrons from all over the world appreciate. ANZU is renowned for an Epicurean ingenuity that is truly captivating – no small feat in San Francisco.

B44
44 Belden Pl., San Francisco: 415- 986-6287
No website
CUISINE: Spanish/ Tapas / Small Plates
DRINKS: Full bar
SERVING: Lunch/Dinner
B44 features a full bar, heated terrace seating with lamps and a canopy. Bistro style seating, very tasty food.

BOURBON STEAK
335 Powell St., San Francisco: 415-397-3003
www.michaenina.net
CUISINE: Steakhouse/ American
DRINKS: Full Bar
SERVING: Dinner
Fresh, seasonal West Coast ingredients. Prior to roasting, all meats are first poached. Chef Michael Mina classics include Braised Short Ribs, Truffled Mac & Cheese, House Steak Burger with Trio of Duck Fat Fries, Classic Cheese Fondue and Maine Lobster Pot Pie. Respecting the room's unique and varied history, designer Michael Dalton blends history with a robust and modern point of view.

CAFE DE LA PRESSE
352 Grant Ave., San Francisco: 415-398-2680
cafedelapresse.com
CUISINE: French/ Continental
DRINKS: Full Bar
SERVING: Lunch/Dinner
Parisian-inspired Cafe de la Presse continues the trend with international literature, classic fare, and the age-old pastime of dining, relaxing, and conversing in a vibrant atmosphere.

COLIBRI MEXICAN BISTRO
438 Geary St., San Francisco: 415-440-2737
colibrimexicanbistro.com
CUISINE: Mexican/ Southwestern
DRINKS: Full Bar
SERVING: Lunch/Dinner
Offers a mix of traditional and diverse Mexican cuisine. The complex flavors from the kitchen are complimented with creative drinks, selected Tequilas, beer and wine from the bar. The decor matches that found in Mexico City's cantinas in the early 1900s. They serve their authentic cuisine in a tapas style so that you can enjoy multiple dishes to share with others.

DAILY GRILL
347 Geary St., San Francisco: 415-616-5000
dailygrill.com
CUISINE: American/ Steakhouse
DRINKS: Full Bar

SERVING: Breakfast/Lunch/Dinner
Located in the heart of bustling Union Square, Daily Grill is an updated version of the San Francisco grills of the past, providing generous portions of classic American dishes, such as steaks, chops, chicken pot pie, and meat loaf... a neat, friendly place where one can get crab cakes or a burger, Shrimp Louie or a T-Bone, along with martinis, single malts, microbrews and a good bottle of wine. The ambience is lively and clubby, with comfortable booths, dark woods and high ceilings.

E&O TRADING COMPANY
314 Sutter St., San Francisco: 415-693-0303
eosanfrancisco.com
CUISINE: Asian / American
DRINKS: Full Bar
SERVING: Lunch/Dinner
Comfy spot with an interesting mix of American and Asian foods: chicken lettuce cups, crispy lemongrass risotto cakes, albacore crudo, great rolls and dumplings (butternut squash dumpling my personal favorite), fresh prawns in lemongrass. Great meat selections: hoisin and coffee glazed spare ribs, Thai-style sliced pork tenderloin, Mongolian lamb stir-fry.

FISH & FARM
339 Taylor St., San Francisco: 415-474-3474
fishandfarmsf.com
CUISINE: Californian/ American
DRINKS: Full Bar
SERVING: Dinner
Only 48 seats in this place with chocolate brown tufted booths, rich bamboo flooring. Organic produce and all sustainably farmed or harvested seafood and meats. Award Winning wine list of 40 world wines under $50 and a limited "Frank's" list of exclusive wines; all from the best producers in the world. With appetizers priced in the $7-$12 range and entrees priced from $16-$28 Fish & Farm offers a clever menu of West Coast seafood and lamb, beef, pork, and artisanal meats from regional small farms. Desserts are variations on American classics. The lounge and bar seats a cozy 20 persons and offers a menu of hand-crafted items.

LARK CREEK STEAK
845 Market St., 4th Floor, San Francisco: 415-593-4100
larkcreeksteak.com
CUISINE: Steakhouse
DRINKS: Full Bar

SERVING: Lunch/Dinner
Inspired by the Bay Area's plentiful bounty of fresh products, Lark Creek Steak offers a menu that is a veritable study in the classic and the new with an abundance of USDA Prime Steaks, fish, vegetable and dessert options to satisfy the palate. Using the best ingredients, Chef Ishmael Macias features seasonally-changing, a-la-carte steakhouse lunch and dinner dishes that are both simply prepared and delectable to taste.

LE COLONIAL
20 Cosmo Pl., San Francisco: 415-931-3600
lecolonialsf.com
CUISINE: Vietnamese/ French
DRINKS: Full Bar
SERVING: Dinner
The aim here is to evoke Excellent Vietnamese cuisine served in a romantic French setting reminiscent of days gone by. Le Colonial evokes the tropical elegance of Vietnam in the 1920s.

MICHAEL MINA
Westin St. Francis Hotel
335 Powell St. (at Geary St.), San Francisco: 415-397-9222
www.michaelmia.net
CUISINE: American
DRINKS: full bar
SERVING: Dinner
The unusual prix-fixe arrangement here appeals to some people, but doesn't appeal to others. That's because you're putting your stomach in the hands of a chef. But I think it's great. Each course comes with the main item prepared in 3 different ways. If one course is lobster, let's say, you'll get it rendered in 3 different styles. So a lot of little bites add up to a very interesting (and wildly diverse) meal. (Sides are as interesting—and as varied—as each course.) Superior wines accompany the meal. Give this place a try: a unique San Francisco experience. (Mina was named Chef of the Year by *Bon Appétit* in 2006.)

MILLENNIUM
Hotel California
580 Geary St., San Francisco: 415-345-3900
millenniumrestaurant.com
CUISINE: Vegetarian / Vegan
DRINKS: Beer
SERVING: Dinner

Millennium, San Francisco's premier vegetarian restaurant, is proud to be regarded as one of the few places to get truly creative food.

NEW DELHI RESTAURANT
160 Ellis St., San Francisco: 415-397-8470
newdelhirestaurant.com
CUISINE: Indian/ Vegetarian
DRINKS: Full Bar
SERVING: Lunch/Dinner
Named one of the finest Indian Restaurants in the U.S. by *The New York Times* and featured on the *Galloping Gourmet* TV show, New Delhi is the place to dine. Decorated like a Maharajah's private banquet room, the restaurant serves cuisine made from recipes culled from the royal Indian menus dating back 300 to 400 years using the freshest local ingredients.

THE ROTUNDA AT NEIMAN MARCUS
150 Stockton St., San Francisco: 415-249-2720
www.opentable.com/the-rotunda-at-neiman-marcus
CUISINE: Contemporary American
DRINKS: Full Bar
SERVING: Lunch/Afternoon Tea
This spectacular restaurant sits underneath a stunning glass dome constructed of more than 2500 pieces of colored glass. The room curves around a central atrium four stories above the entrance. Be sure to request a cozy private booth or a window seat overlooking historic Union Square. Indulge in a glass of bubbles while noshing on their signature Lobster Club or stop by this popular spot to fatten up on the sweets and tea sandwiches during their Afternoon Tea.

STRAITS RESTAURANT
845 Market St., 4th Floor, San Francisco: 415-668-1783
straitsrestaurants.com
CUISINE: Pan-Asian
DRINKS: Full Bar
SERVING: Lunch/Dinner
Singapore for almost 200 years has been at the crossroads of Southeast Asia, where many cultures and nationalities live, work and more importantly, eat together. Singapore's cuisines logically reflect this cultural diversity. The four major culinary cultures -- Malaysian/Indonesian, Chinese, Indian and Nonya -- are in fact a blend of each other, creating a new cuisine that is unique and more complex in flavors and fragrances.

Straits Restaurant offers a menu that features the complexity of all these Singaporean cuisines in chef Chris Yeo's unique interpretation.

THE CASTRO

The Castro District, commonly known as The Castro (coined by gay activist speaker Neil Davendra Vyas), within Eureka Valley in San Francisco, is widely considered America's first, currently largest, and best-known gay neighborhood.

BACCO RISTORANTE
737 Diamond St., San Francisco: 415-282-4969
baccosf.com
CUISINE: Italian
DRINKS: Beer/ Wine
SERVING: Dinner
"When you pull back the curtain at the door of Bacco, you enter into a decidedly Italian world. Since it opened in 1993, Chef Vincenzo Cucco has been turning out delicious food, some of the best made to order risotto, pastas, etc. In all, Bacco is a top neighborhood restaurant and truly offers a meal to savor." -Michael Bauer, *S.F Chronicle* restaurant critic

BISOU
2367 Market St., San Francisco: 415-556-6200
bisoubistro.com
CUISINE: French
DRINKS: Beer
SERVING: Dinner
Situated in the heart of the Castro (at Market and Castro St.), Bisou, "petit baiser", in English "Kiss" is bringing traditional French cuisine in a new style and based on locally and organically grown products. Bisou offers dinner and weekend brunch menus, but also provides late-night dinner that pairs well with a delicious cocktail or glass of wine.

HAIGHT-ASHBURY

One of the funkier neighborhoods in all San Francisco, it's definitely very colorful.

CHA CHA CHA
1801 Haight St. (at Shrader St.), San Francisco: 415-386-7670; also in The Mission at 2327 Mission St. (bet. 19th and 20th), 415-648-0504, but dinner only.
www.cha3.com

CUISINE: Caribbean
DRINKS: beer & wine (get the Sangria)
SERVING: lunch & dinner on Haight; dinner only in The Mission
Busy as hell at night, but that's really part of the fun here. You'll have to wait for a table; no reservations. Order tapas style from a menu including black mussels, Cajun shrimp, seafood paella, arroz con pollo, lechon asado, jerk chicken. It's reasonably priced and lots of fun, but LOUD. (Lunch is quieter.)

KAN ZAMAN
1793 Haight St., San Francisco: 415-751-9656
CUISINE: Middle Eastern
DRINKS: full bar
SERVING: dinner weekdays; lunch & dinner weekends
www.kanzamansf.com
One of the weirdest places you've ever been. They'll certainly keep you busy with the belly dancers (Thursday-Saturday only from 9 p.m.; check to be sure), the exotic Middle Eastern food, the hookah pipe (you actually smoke a fruit-based "tobacco," not the real thing). You have to sit cross-legged at low tables for the whole experience. Another thing: it's very cheap.

FISHERMANS WHARF
Roughly encompasses the northern waterfront area of San Francisco from Ghirardelli Square or Van Ness Avenue east to Pier 35 or Kearny Street. The F Market streetcar runs through the area, the Powell-Hyde cable car lines runs to Aquatic Park, at the edge of Fisherman's Wharf, and the Powell-Mason cable car line runs a few blocks away.

ALIOTO'S
#8 Fisherman's Wharf, San Francisco: 415- 673-0183
aliotos.com
CUISINE: Seafood/ Italian
DRINKS: Full bar
SERVING: Lunch/Dinner
Alioto's Italian Seafood Restaurant is located in the heart of San Francisco's famed Fisherman's Wharf overlooking the historic fishing fleet and the Golden Gate Bridge. The Alioto family has been serving local seafood at the same location for the past 85 years. The recently remodeled restaurant features a warm ambiance with a 3-tiered dining room offering every guest stunning views of San Francisco Bay. Classic menu. Don't

forget to try their world-famous cioppino and Dungeness crab, always fresh.

CAFE PESCATORE
2455 Mason St., San Francisco: 415-561-1111
cafepescatore.com
CUISINE: Italian/ Seafood
DRINKS: Beer
SERVING: Breakfast/Lunch/Dinner
Cafe Pescatore is the perfect neighborhood sidewalk cafe serving Italian specialties and wood oven pizzas with an emphasis on fresh seafood.

CRAB HOUSE AT PIER 39
203C Pier 39, San Francisco: 415-434-2722
crabhouse39.com
CUISINE: Seafood/ American
DRINKS: Full Bar
SERVING: Lunch/Dinner
Voted "best crab in San Francisco", this cozy, wood-paneled boathouse is home of the world famous Killer Crab (R), over two pounds of roasted whole Dungeness crab. Other specialties include sizzling iron skillet-roasted mussels, shrimp and crab, crab enchiladas, crab cioppino, crab angel hair lasagna, hot crab melt sandwich, seared filet mignon and lobster thermidor.

GARY DANKO
800 North Point St. (at Hyde St.), San Francisco: 415-749-2060
www.garydanko.com
CUISINE: French
DRINKS: Full bar
SERVING: Dinner
While the food will remind you of some of the best *haute cuisine* you've ever had, the ambience in which it's served is much more casual than you'd expect. This is another (how many are there, you wonder?) one of those dining "musts" you have to experience in San Francisco. The *prix fixe* arrangement here gives you a choice of 3 or 4 or 5 courses. (The wines I find are in the "ripoff" category—way too high, so I always struggle to find something reasonable.) One of the problems here is actually getting a seat. You simply *must* reserve a table. If you are just 2 persons (or by yourself), then go early and nab one of the 10 or 12 bar seats where you don't need a reservation. You can eat at the bar. I love this bar. It's great fun, and you get to meet people you wouldn't otherwise if you were stuck at a table.

Danko is a James Beard Award Winning Chef, and after you walk out of this place, you won't find that a surprise.

SCOMA
Pier 47 & Al Scoma Way (bet. Jefferson & Jones), San Francisco: 415-771-4383
www.scomas.com
If you've never been to San Francisco, this is the kind of place that probably comes to mind when you think of Fisherman's Wharf. Before the Gary Dankos of the world brought a little class into the neighborhood, this is what it was like. And out-of-towners flock here, where the portions are huge and the food is basic. It's not fancy seafood, just the traditional seafood menu you'd find anywhere else. But it's really good, and you get the picture-perfect waterfront views. But listen, it's NOT CHEAP. Like any other tourist trap, it's not free. (For the same money, you could go to a really fine eatery and experience something really special.)

THE MISSION

BABY BLUES BBQ
3149 Mission St., San Francisco: 415-896-4250
babybluessf.com
CUISINE: Barbecue/ American
DRINKS: Beer
SERVING: Lunch/Dinner
The best damn BBQ in San Francisco. They slow smoke their meats to delicious perfection. They offer three different styles of ribs including Baby Backs, Memphis Style long bone, and the Texas style beef rib. Yummy :) Both their pulled pork and beef brisket are braised in Guinness. They have a variety of fixin's including collard greens, mac-n-cheese, baked beans, sauteed okra, potato salad, and many, many more.

BLOWFISH SUSHI TO DIE FOR
2170 Bryant St., San Francisco: 415-285-3848
blowfishsushi.com
CUISINE: Sushi/ Asian
DRINKS: Full Bar
SERVING: Lunch/Dinner
Blowfish Sushi is an eclectic sushi bar and restaurant that serves both modern and traditional sushi, and sashimi, as well as salads, cooked

appetizers and special desserts. The menu style is Asian Fusion and emphasizes clean, pure healthy foods.

CENTRAL KITCHEN
3000 20th St. (between Alabama & Florida Sts.), San Francisco: 415-826-7004
www.centralkitchensf.com/
CUISINE: New American
DRINKS: beer & wine
SERVING: dinner only from 5:30.
Cutting edge cuisine from the same people that brought you **Flour & Water.** Here you'll want to try the crispy goat and quinoa fritters, pork cracklings with lime, chanterelle soup with sunchokes, nettles, hen with oysters, lettuce and smoked tomato. (They share a courtyard with another restaurant, **Salumeria**, which is open from 9 to 7.)

COMMONWEALTH
2224 Mission St., San Francisco: 415-355-1500
commonwealthsf.com
CUISINE: American
DRINKS: Beer/ Wine
SERVING: Lunch/Dinner
There's a big emphasis here on pairing the food with wine. (And the selections are excellent.) I suggest you opt for the 6-course tasting menu (it's $65 and the items change constantly). If you do, $10 goes to a local charity. Now, that's "giving back." Even if you get the tasting menu, order the sweetbreads on the side. Simply succulent. Semifinalist for the Beard Award for Best New Restaurant in 2011.

FARINA
3560 18th St., San Francisco: 415-565-0360
farina-foods.com
CUISINE: Italian
DRINKS: Full Bar
SERVING: Dinner
At Farina you can admire the daily preparation of freshly homemade pastas, enjoying the tasteful "focaccia di Recco" while sipping a glass of Pigato wine or one of their specialty cocktails.

FLOUR + WATER
2401 Harrison St. (between 20th & 21st Sts.), San Francisco: 415-826-7000

flourandwater.com
You'd never know it, but this is one of the hottest spots in San Francisco right now. Homemade pasta, pizzas, sandwiches and just all-around excellent Italian fare served up quickly in a bustling environment.

LOVEJOY'S TEA ROOM
1351 Church St. ((bet. Clipper St. & 26th St.), San Francisco: 415-648-5895
www.lovejoystearoom.com
This lovely little spot is really in the Noe Valley district adjacent to The Mission, but I am putting it here for now. Quite a different sort of "high tea" with things like artichoke hummus, cream cheese and jam sandwiches with no crust (the way Grandma used to make 'em). Scones, crumpets, nice sandwiches, salads and pub food. None of the china matches and they have a wide range of organic teas. Sweets are excellent.

MISSION CHINESE FOOD
LUNG SHAN CHINESE RESTAURANT
2234 Mission St., San Francisco: 415-863-2800
CUISINE: Chinese
DRINKS: Beer/ Wine
SERVING: Lunch/ Dinner
missionchinesefood.com
Noted for spiciness of its food. This is really 2 restaurants in 1. Tea-smoked eel ($9), pig ear terrine ($7), Ma Po Tofu ($11, pork shoulder with Szechuan peppercorns), salt cod fried rice ($10, with Chinese sausage, eggs, scallions). **Commonwealth** (see listing), got the idea of donating a portion of each sale to charity from this place.

SALUMERIA
3000 20th St. (between Alabama & Florida Sts.), San Francisco: 415-471-2998
www.salumeriasf.com
A super deli with great meats and cheese and sandwiches and oils and gift items and, well, everything. Great spot for a lovely meal.

TSUNAMI
301 King St., #B, San Francisco: 415-284-0111
dajanigroup.net
CUISINE: Sushi/ Japanese
DRINKS: Full Bar
SERVING: Lunch/Dinner

Tsunami Mission Bay located at the corner of 4th & Berry provides a young, hip and exciting restaurant experience. Tsunami Mission Bay combines the best of both - Nihon and Tsunami Panhandle - using Nihon's extensive selection of spirits; and incorporating the culinary influence from Tsunami Panhandle. An amazing Sake list is also offered.

VEGA
419 Cortland Ave., San Francisco: 415-285-6000
vegapizzasf.com
CUISINE: Italian
DRINKS: Beer/Wine
SERVING: Dinner
Husband/wife duo, Giuseppe Manna from Rome, Italy and Vega Freeman-Brady from Berkeley, CA have created a warm, cozy restaurant where friends and neighbors enjoy homemade gnocchi, pastas, bread and thin crust pizzas all made with local, fresh, seasonal ingredients. Everything from the bread to the deserts are made in house from family recipes.

NOB HILL

Nob Hill is one of San Francisco's signature neighborhoods. In addition to its swanky character, the area is influenced by the diverse personalities of the downtown neighborhoods that surround it, making it an intriguing place to visit.

The area's reputation of privilege dates back to Gold Rush times, when cable car lines made the hilltop accessible and the railroad barons and bonanza kings built their mansions there.

BIG 4 RESTAURANT
1075 California St., San Francisco: 415-474-5400
big4restaurant.com
CUISINE: American
DRINKS: Full Bar
SERVING: Breakfast/ Dinner
It takes its name from the four powerful storied railroad tycoons of San Francisco history, and has a suitably old-boys-club feeling, with dark wood paneling and memorabilia on the walls. The menu does feature the big steaks you'd expect at a place like this, as well as the occasional wild game entrée special, but also makes room for creative contemporary dishes. With nightly piano music in the bar.

GRUBSTAKE
1525 Pine St., San Francisco: 415-673-8268
sfgrubstake.com
CUISINE: American Diner
DRINKS: Beer/ Wine
SERVING: Dinner/ Late night/ Breakfast on weekends
Though at heart it's simply a diner, there's a lot that stands out about Grubstake, not least its memorable name. Part of the restaurant is housed in a rail car, a remnant of the Key Line, and the menu lists a number of Portuguese dishes along with its burgers, milkshakes and breakfast fare. Best of all, considering its proximity to the Polk St. night spots, it's open until 4 a.m.

HOUSE OF PRIME RIB
1906 Van Ness Ave., San Francisco: 415-885-4605
www.houseofprimerib.net
CUISINE: American Steakhouse
DRINKS: Full Bar
SERVING: Dinner
Anthony Bourdain says he loves this place because it's a little old-fashioned, even tacky (flocked wallpaper), but they "serve you martinis you can swim in." The beef? Just perfectly delicious.

LE COLONIAL
20 Cosmo Pl., San Francisco: 415-931-3600
lecolonialsf.com
CUISINE: Vietnamese
DRINKS: Full Bar
SERVING: Dinner/ Lunch on weekends only
Le Colonial isn't a place to hurry. The sexy, plantation-style surroundings are designed to be soothing and to promote lively conversations, fueled by some exotic drinks and innovative food. Main courses start at $23 for lemongrass roasted chicken and rise to $33 for the grilled lamb chops. Sea bass in banana leaves and crisp spring rolls are classics, while the duck is an exceptional new addition to the menu. The dessert fondue with rum makes a light-but-indulgent ending.

SWAN OYSTER DEPOT
1517 Polk St., San Francisco: 415-673-1101
No Website
CUISINE: Seafood
DRINKS: Beer/ Wine

SERVING: Lunch; closes at 5:30 p.m.
This venerable seafood counter has been in business since 1912, and owned by the Sancimino family since 1946: it's safe to say Swan knows its daily catch. Pull up a stool (or wait in line for one), and feast like a king in this eminently casual establishment, where the only seating is a marble counter stocked with lemon wedges, Tabasco sauce, oyster crackers, and other seafood essentials. Choose from seafood salads and cocktails, lobster, Dungeness crab and, of course, Swan's signature mollusk. You can also pick up some fresh fish to cook at home. Note: closes at 5:30 pm.

RUSSIAN HILL

Russian Hill, a residential neighborhood with pockets of restaurants and shops, feels a bit more visitor-friendly than its more formal neighbor, Nob Hill. The views are also just as dazzling.

The center of Russian Hill is accessible by the Hyde-Powell cable car and two Muni buses, the 41 (weekday rush hour only) and the 45. The 19 runs along Polk Street, stopping frequently from Ghirardelli Square to the Tenderloin.

ACQUERELLO
1722 Sacramento St., San Francisco: 415-567-5432
acquerello.com
CUISINE: Italian
DRINKS: Full Bar
SERVING: Dinner
Acquerello, named for its original watercolors, envelops guests in a warm and gracious atmosphere the moment they arrive. A recent renovation of the 20-year old restaurant, led by designer John Wheatman, highlights the former chapel, graced with arches and a rustic wood-beamed vaulted ceiling, with warm Mediterranean colors of gold and terracotta. The 50 seat dining room is softly illuminated with light from polished brass lamps which dances off an extensive collection of crystal decanters and a large floral bouquet greeting guests as they enter. Co-owners Giancarlo Paterlini and Suzette Gresham-Tognetti work together to provide an unparallel Italian dining experience.

LA FOLIE
2316 Polk St., San Francisco: 415-776-5577
lafolie.com
CUISINE: French

DRINKS: Full Bar
SERVING: Dinner
La Folie is a French restaurant located in Russian Hill of San Francisco. Chef Roland Passot, with his wife Jamie opened La Folie in March of 1988. He combines the freshest ingredients in exotic combinations. Each plate leaves the kitchen resembling art-a canvas of color and design that tastes even better than it looks. La Folie continues to be rated as one of the top restaurants, receiving a star from the *Michelin Guide*, 4 stars from the *San Francisco Chronicle* and 4 stars from *San Francisco* magazine.

RISTORANTE MILANO
1448 Pacific Ave., San Francisco: 415-673-2961
milanosf.com
CUISINE: Italian/ Seafood
DRINKS: Beer
SERVING: Dinner
The flavors of Milano's food and the rhythm of the dining room are reminiscent of trattorias in Italy, according to Gourmet Magazine. It is a charming, intimate restaurant with an Italian staff, top quality ingredients, homemade pastas, exceptional veal, polenta, risotto, and fresh seafood delivered daily, served in warm surroundings. Known as the "hidden jewel of Russian Hill," the *San Francisco Chronicle* calls Milano "one of the most consistent restaurants in the city."

CIVIC CENTER
Small area a few blocks north of the intersection of Market Street and Van Ness Avenue that's home to the big government and cultural institutions.

ABSINTHE BRASSERIE AND BAR
398 Hayes St., San Francisco: 415-551-1590
absinthe.com
CUISINE: French/ Californian
DRINKS: Full Bar
SERVING: Dinner
Absinthe Brasserie and Bar is a Hayes Valley hot spot with upscale bistro fare and popular bar within walking distance to the performing arts centers.

ALAMO SQUARE SEAFOOD GRILL
803 Fillmore St., San Francisco: 415-440-2828
alamosquareseafoodgrill.com
CUISINE: Seafood/ French

DRINKS: Beer
SERVING: Dinner
They specialize in fresh seafood served up in generous portions. On Wednesday you can "Bring Your Own Wine" and they waive the corkage fee. Known as a neighborhood favorite where the food's good and the prices fair. Snapper, salmon, tuna, swordfish, petrale sole are all priced very reasonably, especially when you consider all the side dishes they include.

PACIFIC HEIGHTS

Pacific Heights is located in one of the most scenic and park-like settings in Northern California, offering panoramic views of the Golden Gate Bridge, the San Francisco Bay, Alcatraz and the Presidio. Its idyllic location provides a temperate micro-climate that is clearer, but not always warmer, than many other areas in San Francisco.

1300 ON FILLMORE
1300 Fillmore St., San Francisco: 415-771-7100
1300fillmore.com
CUISINE: American/ Californian
DRINKS: Full Bar
SERVING: Dinner/Sunday Gospel brunch
1300 on Fillmore is a restaurant and lounge that draws on the rich cultural history of San Francisco's Fillmore Jazz District. The restaurant serves "Soulful American" Cuisine, accompanied by a list of the finest California wines. Soulful American Cuisine prepared as interpreted by internationally recognized chef David Lawrence. Lawrence combines classic French cooking techniques with hints of southern flavors using fresh, California seasonal ingredients.

SOMA

Most of the action can be found in three general areas: by South Park and the Giants ballpark, around the San Francisco MOMA and Yerba Buena gardens, and over by Folsom and Eleventh Street. SoMa, as it's known, sounds a little like a SoHo wannabe, and it does have a strong downtown vibe.

ALEXANDER'S STEAKHOUSE
448 Brannan St., San Francisco: 415- 495-1111
alexanderssteakhouse.com

CUISINE: Steakhouse/ Asian
DRINKS: Full Bar
SERVING: Dinner
San Francisco is the second installment of Alexander's Steakhouse which is a privately invested corporation operated under direction of Executive Chef, Jeffrey Stout. Located in the SOMA district of the city near AT&T Park, Alexander's Steakhouse is a welcome addition to the city dining scene offering a fine dining interpretation of the classic American steakhouse with hints of Japanese influence throughout the menu. Featuring a variety of classic cuts such as Porterhouse, T-bone and New York, they specialize in Prime Certified Angus Beef grain-fed from the Mid-West.

BASIL CANTEEN
1489 Folsom St., San Francisco: 415-552-3963
www.basilthai.com
CUISINE: Thai/ Asian/ Tapas/ Small Plates
DRINKS: Full bar
SERVING: Lunch/Dinner
Here you'll find the flavors of Bangkok and the atmosphere of the old landmark 'Jackson Brewery' in SOMA. Wide range of Thai snacks, noodles, rice dishes, special house cocktails. They have a long communal table or you can opt for a table in their sometimes cramped mezzanine.

BENU
22 Hawthorne St., San Francisco: 415-685-4860
benusf.com
CUISINE: American
DRINKS: Beer/ Wine.
SERVING: Dinner
Chef David Chang calls Benu "the best restaurant in America" because Korean-born Chef Corey Lee has not only fused Asian and European cuisines (one dish is risotto with sea urchin, pumpkin, lovage, black truffle, for instance), but also "modernized" tradition-bound Asian culinary customs. No small feat. The result is sublime.
Expect dishes like pork rib with carrot, jujube, endive, black sesame, spices ($28), beef braised in pear, king trumpet mushroom, sunflower seeds and leaves ($32), steamed bass with crispy skin, gai choy, turnip, mustard seed ($28). Benu offers two dining options: an à la carte menu and a tasting menu. The à la carte menu allows you to range all over, but if it's your first time, go with the tasting menu. You'll get to experience this dynamic cuisine. Chef Lee used to work for Thomas Keller in New York when he

was chef du cuisine at the French Laundry. On weekends, plan to reserve couple of months ahead; weekdays a week ahead.

Benu is housed in a historic building in the heart of San Francisco's SOMA district. The restaurant is within walking distance of the Moscone Center, the San Francisco Museum of Modern Art, Yerba Buena Gardens, the Contemporary Jewish Museum and many hotels including the St. Regis, W, Four Seasons and The Palace.

KOH SAMUI & THE MONKEY
415 Brannan St., San Francisco: 415-369-0007
kohsamuiandthemonkey.com
CUISINE: Thai/ Vegetarian
DRINKS: Full Bar
SERVING: Lunch/Dinner
This hip, award-winning restaurant in SOMA features traditional Thai food influenced by the owner's extensive traveling. Extensive beer, wine and sake list.

TRIPTYCH
1155 Folsom St., San Francisco: 415-703-0557
triptychsf.com
CUISINE: American/ Californian
DRINKS: Full Bar
SERVING: Lunch/Dinner
Triptych's South of Market location embraces the industrial with the arts culture of the neighborhood. The cuisine reflects the diverse palates of its patrons and is complimented by a unique wine list from around the world. Local artists' works are displayed. Triptych is an oasis of cuisine, culture, and ambiance.

MARINA
The neighborhood is most famous for the Palace of Fine Arts, which shelters the Exploratorium, a renowned hands-on science museum and children's educational center, and which takes up much of the western section of the neighborhood. The Palace is the only building left standing in its original location within the 1915 Exposition fairgrounds. The grounds around the Palace are a popular year-round attraction for tourists and locals, and are a favorite location for weddings and wedding party photographs for couples.

ALEGRIAS FOOD FROM SPAIN
2018 Lombard St., San Francisco: 415- 929-8888

alegriassf.com
CUISINE: Spanish/ Tapas / Small Plates
DRINKS: Beer/Wine
SERVING: Dinner
Alegrias on Lombard Street offers more than 20 kinds of small plates as well as a short wine list mostly featuring selections from Spain. The restaurant is run by the Faedi Gonzalez family and has homespun warmth. Framed family photographs and Spanish travel posters adorn the walls in the two dining rooms.

BAKER STREET BISTRO
2953 Baker St., San Francisco: 415-931-1475
bakerstreetbistro.com
CUISINE: French
DRINKS: Beer
SERVING: Lunch/Dinner/Brunch
Serving up authentic French cuisine, Baker Street Bistro has been a neighborhood gem for nearly two decades. Pull up a chair on their sun-drenched patio for a leisurely weekend brunch or escape the San Francisco fog in the intimate dining room for a romantic dinner.
Their extensive bistro menu includes French classics such as the Bourride (a rich seafood stew), Duck Confit, and Grilled Lamb Chops. Locals and French ex-pats alike swear by the fresh daily specials, Moules Provençale (mussels in white wine, shallots, parsley, tomato & pesto) and Pain Perdu (fluffy, melt-in-your-mouth cinnamon French toast). Owner & Executive Chef Danel de Betelu brings a taste of his homeland to Cow Hollow. He leads a warm and welcoming staff who all share a passion for great food.

NORTH BEACH

North Beach is a neighborhood in the northeast of San Francisco adjacent to Chinatown, Fisherman's Wharf and Russian Hill. The neighborhood is San Francisco's Little Italy, and has historically been home to a large Italian American population. It still holds many Italian restaurants today, though many other ethnic groups currently live in the neighborhood. It was also the historic center of the beatnik subculture. Today, North Beach is one of San Francisco's main red light and nightlife districts as well as a residential neighborhood populated by a mix of young urban professionals, families and Chinese immigrants connected to the adjacent Chinatown. **(NOTE: there are many bars with really excellent food that could easily be listed in the restaurant section, but we have put them in the Nightlife section because the primary focus is on the bar.)**

ALBONA RISTORANTE ISTRIANO
545 Francisco St., San Francisco: 415-441-1040
albonarestaurant.com
CUISINE: European/ Italian
DRINKS: Full Bar
SERVING: Dinner
Bruno Viscovi came to America from the hillside town of Albona, overlooking the Istrian Peninsula on the Adriatic Sea, located just southeast of Trieste on the borders of Italy, Slovenia, and Croatia. The memories of his palate are distinctively expressed with the only Istrian Menu on the West Coast. The unusual dishes and recipes of his region reflect the infusions from the Italians, Austrians, Hungarians, Slavs, Spaniards, French, Jews, Greeks, and Turks. In 2008 Bruno retired. His executive chef, Samuel Hernandez, now runs the restaurant. Excellent reviews have appeared in many publications including the list of The Bay Area's Top 100 Restaurants for eight consecutive years, Zagat, and the Michelin Guide.

CAPP'S CORNER
1600 Powell St., San Francisco: 415-989-2589
www.cappscorner.com
If you've got a large family, this is the place to bring them for huge piles of good Italian food that won't break the bank. Tables are long for family-style seating. Selections are your basic Italian time-tested favorites: spaghetti and meatballs, pasta with shrimp, osso buco, leg of lamb. Sassy waitresses who look (and act) like they belong in a diner are fun to watch work.

MAYKADEH
470 Green St., San Francisco: 415-362-8286
maykadehrestaurant.com
CUISINE: Persian/ Middle Eastern/ Vegetarian
DRINKS: Full Bar
SERVING: Lunch/Dinner
Welcome to Maykadeh Restaurant, where Persian tradition and a thousand years of history come together and creates one of the most unique restaurants in North America. They also serve halal food.

SUNSET DISTRICT

The Sunset District contains many large park and recreation areas. The San Francisco Zoo is located in the southwestern corner of the neighborhood by Lake Merced, the largest lake within San Francisco. Also within the Lake Merced area are two large golf courses, the private Olympic

Club and San Francisco Golf Club, and the public TPC Harding Park. Across from Lake Merced is Fort Funston, an old coastal battery, now part of the Golden Gate National Recreation Area.

BEACH CHALET BREWERY & RESTAURANT
1000 Great Hwy., San Francisco: 415-386-8439
beachchalet.com
CUISINE: American/ Brewery/ Seafood
DRINKS: Full bar
SERVING: Breakfast/Lunch/Dinner
The Beach Chalet Brewery and Restaurant is located in San Francisco's Golden Gate Park where the park meets the Pacific Ocean. They feature a spectacular ocean view, handcrafted beer, full bar and free parking. They serve a modern American menu for breakfast, lunch and dinner daily. Try their 3-6-9 Happy Hour Monday to Friday 3pm to 6pm and 9pm to close they serve a menu of drinks and appetizers that are $3, $6 or $9 for you to enjoy. Other specials include: Prime Rib on Monday nights and Brunch a la Carte Saturdays and Sundays 8am to 2pm.

Chapter 4
NIGHTLIFE

NORTH BEACH

15 ROMOLO
15 Romolo Place, San Francisco: 415-398-1359
www.15romolo.com
A really fun place that also has quite good bar food (excellent hot dogs and burgers, top quality ingredients).

AMANTE
570 Green St., San Francisco: 415-362-4400
http://www.amantesf.com
Chill atmosphere and great people watching. Nothing fancy but really cool. Service is fast and friendly. Great martinis.

ANTOLOGIA VINOTECA
515 Broadway, San Francisco: 415-274-8423
http://antologiasf.com/
It's easy to like the food here (get the fig flatbread) as well as the extensive selection of wines from Latin America (one of the few places in this wine-centic city that specializes in wines from Spain, Central and South America). Brazilian and Mexican music on the weekends.

BIMBO'S 365 CLUB
1025 Columbus Ave., San Francisco: 415-474-0365
http://www.bimbos365club.com
Great space with a dance floor and stage. They usually have pretty decent bands playing. Parking might be a challenge. The drinks are good and their prices are average.

BOTTLE CAP
1707 Powell St., San Francisco: 415-529-2237
www.bottlecapsf.com/

Yes, the fun bar is the main attraction, but you'll swoon over some of the food. Try the seared scallops with quinoa green-onion cake, red onion jam and a side fennel salad ($10), or the fried chicken thighs with fresh dill yogurt, $8. Great happy hour specials till 7. A jazz pianist keeps things hopping from 7 to 10.

CHURCH KEY
1402 Grant Ave., San Francisco: 415-963-1713
NO WEBSITE
Amazing beer selection and some really cool people in this place. No cover and totally unpretentious. (People come from all over to sample the rare beers they have in stock.)

GINO & CARLO COCKTAIL LOUNGE
548 Green St., San Francisco: 415-421-0896
NO WEBSITE
You'll probably walk into this place and find a lot of people having a really good time. The bartenders make sure that the drinks are flowing and that makes everybody happy.

ROSEWOOD
732 Broadway, San Francisco: 415-951-4886
http://www.rosewoodbar.com
Clean, sleek and modern. It doesn't get too crowded and the DJ will take requests. Drinks can be pricey but overall good place.

SIP BAR & LOUNGE
787 Broadway St., San Francisco: 415-699-6545
http://www.siploungesf.com
No cover, decently priced drinks and good pours. Friendly, good looking bartenders and good music.

VESUVIO
255 Columbus Ave., San Francisco: 415-362-3370
http://www.vesuvio.com
Walk in through these doors and get ready to experience the writers, artists, bohemians and intellects that frequent this cool place. Great atmosphere , reasonably priced drinks and the bartenders have great San Francisco stories.

FINANCIAL DISTRICT

BAMBOO HUT
479 Broadway, San Francisco: 415-989-8555
NO WEBSITE
Tiki inspired bar, DJ, limbo contest and leis. Two great drinks in this place, the pina coladas and their very own volcano bowl. Atmosphere is pretty chill.

EZ5
684 Commercial St., San Francisco: 415-362-9321
http://www.ez5bar.com
Divey bar but with lots of character. DJ's in back playing a good variety of music. Usually not that crowded so it's comfortable and the service is quick. Not bad drink prices either.

GRASSLANDS BAR & LOUNGE
905 Kearny St., San Francisco: 415-288-8636
NO WEBSITE
Newly remodeled, this place is small but cozy. The crowd is mostly professional, $15 credit card minimum.

THE HIDDEN VINE
408 Merchant St., San Francisco: 415-674-3567
http://www.thehiddenvine.com
Great place for happy hour, but get here early because the place gets packed. Atmosphere is dark and moody and they play great 80's music.

THE OCCIDENTAL CIGAR CLUB
471 Pine St., San Francisco: 415-834-0485
http://www.occidentalcigarclub.com
Good ole fashioned cigar smoking bar. Good selection of wines and beers and of course, whiskeys. Selection of cigars might be considered by some as limited.

THE PUNCHLINE
444 Battery St., San Francisco: 415-397-7573
http://www.punchlinecomedyclub.com
They have a lineup of usually good comedians. The venue is a little small but that only means there are no bad seats in the house. Standard 2 drink minimum and staff is friendly.

RICKHOUSE
246 Kearny St., San Francisco: 415-398-2827
http://www.rickhousebar.com
Speakeasy-type of bar with great specialty drinks. Usually has a good size crowd and the service is good.

HAIGHT-ASHBURY

AUB ZAM ZAM
1633 Haight St., San Francisco: 415-861-2545
NO WEBSITE
Interesting, unpretentious little bar with a great vibe. The jukebox is all jazz and 50's music mixed in with a little Tom Waite. The drinks are cheap and they make a mean Martini.

GOLD CANE COCKTAIL LOUNGE
1569 Haight St., San Francisco: 415-626-1112
NO WEBSITE
Total dive bar. Simple, casual and relaxing. Pool table, cheap drinks and a great outdoor patio.

HOBSON'S CHOICE
1601 Haight St., San Francisco: 415-621-5859
http://www.hobsonschoice.com
Usually a nice mixed crowd in good spirits. Very large selection of rums but their specialty is their punch. Fun bar with friendly bartenders in a good location.

KEZAR PUB & RESTAURANT
770 Stanyan St., San Francisco: 415-386-9292
http://www.thekezarpub.com
Great place to catch a game, any game. From pro to college, they will be playing it. Drink prices are standard and their chicken wings have been voted best in the city by the Chronicle.

LITTLE MINSKYS BURLESQUE
Club Deluxe
1511 Haight St., San Francisco: 415-552-6949
NO WEBSITE
Great vintage style burlesque: classy, sexy and sultry. The drinks are stiff, strong and cheap.

THE MILK BAR
1840 Haight St., San Francisco: 415-387-6455
http://www.milksf.com
Nice bar with live music and dance floor. There usually will be a cover charge, regardless of how many people are actually in the place. Friendly bartenders.

MURIO'S TROPHY ROOM
1811 Haight St., San Francisco: 415-752-2971
www.muriostrophyroom.com
One of the last of the true dives in the Haight. Edgy at times, won't meet any trophies here, but overall, truly a great and fun place. Pool table with some excellent shooters.

THE MISSION

500 CLUB
500 Guerrero St., San Francisco: 415-861-2500
http://www.500clubsf.com
Decently poured drinks and friendly bartenders. Big screen TV's for the sports lovers. Karaoke on Sundays and they make a good bloody mary.

THE ATTIC CLUB
3336 24th St., San Francisco: 415-643-3376
NO WEBSITE
Great little dive bar where you can just sit and enjoy the cheap drinks and the people watching. Very interesting crowd that comes and goes. Just be careful of the blonde bartender with the ponytail, she's mean.

BLIND CAT
3050 24th St., San Francisco: 415-401-8474
NO WEBSITE
Cool local watering hole. Dark and rustic with a variety of characters and a good juke box.

BRUNO'S
2389 Mission St., San Francisco: 415-643-5200
http://www.brunossf.com
Friendly staff and a decent crowd. The diversity here is great; you'll find a good fun mix of multiple ethnicities

CIRCOLO
500 Florida St., San Francisco: 415-553-8560
http://www.circolosf.com
Seems about the best thing here is their SoulKrush parties with incredible, high-energy dance music. The food can be hit or miss but they have plenty of free street parking.

DOC'S CLOCK
2575 Mission St., San Francisco: 415-824-3627
http://www.docsclock.com
Nice beer selection in a nice bar with stiff drinks. Great assortment of organic tequilas. Friendly staff, cash only bar.

DOVRE CLUB
1498 Valencia St., San Francisco: 415-285-4169
NO WEBSITE
If you're into dive bars, this is the place for you. Cheap drinks and a decent selection of beer on tap. They have a pool table and are even dog friendly. Cash only bar.

LITTLE BAOBAB
3388 19th St., San Francisco: 415-643-3558
http://www.bissapbaobab.com
Little dance place with a cool African vibe. Some people like the sketchiness and some people don't.

LONE PALM
3394 22nd St., San Francisco: 415-648-0109
No website
Chill little dive bar with good drinks. And yes, those are white tablecloths. Very interesting.

PHOENIX BAR & IRISH GATHERING HOUSE
811 Valencia St., San Francisco: 415-695-1811
http://www.phoenixirishbar.com
Great place to catch any game. Great Irish breakfast, at any time. Cheap happy hour 5-7.

VERDI CLUB
2424 Mariposa St., San Francisco: 415-861-9199
http://www.verdiclub.net

Good sized dance floor and people of all ages and attire mixing it up on the floor. Great place for swing lessons and dancing. Sunday nights they offer Jazz, R&B, Funk, Old School and Blues type music.

SOMA

111 MINNA GALLERY
111 Minna St., San Francisco: 415-974-1719
http://www.111minnagallery.com
Hip-hop and dance music among art. Cool vibe with a very interesting crowd.

83 PROOF
83 1st St., San Francisco: 415-296-8383
http://www.83proof.com
Excellent bar that is well stocked and bartenders that make excellent drinks. Welcoming and friendly, $10 credit card minimum.

BOOTIE AT DNA LOUNGE
375 11th St., San Francisco: 415-626-1409
http://www.bootiesf.com
Club that takes dancing seriously. $10 cover before 10 pm, $15 after. Cash bar only.

BUTTER
354 11th St., San Francisco: 415-863-5964
http://www.smoothasbutter.com
Great dancing music and a fun place to meet a friend for a drink. Very fun place and you must try their tater tots drenched in cheese.

CAT CLUB
1190 Folsom St., San Francisco: 415-703-8965
http://www.sfcatclub.com
Themed music nights, 80's, 90's , etc. People seem to like the 80's night but not much else. Terrible beer selection and over priced drinks. Cover after 9 pm.

THE COSMOPOLITAN
121 Spear St., San Francisco; 415-543-4001
http://www.cosmopolitansf.com

Great place for happy hour. Serving up a mean cosmo, they have have a light happy hour menu. Nice, low-key ambiance.

THE ENDUP
401 6th St., San Francisco: 415-896-1075
http://www.theendup.com
It's a $20 cover, but the place is open until 6 am. Saturday nights are great. Be prepared to get checked for drugs.

EVE
575 Howard St., San Francisco: 415-543-5874
http://www.eveloungesf.com
A lounge, but there are DJ's playing awesome music and a dance floor should you get the urge. Drinks are on the expensive side. On the smaller side, this place can get really loud if crowded.

HARLOT
46 Minna St., San Francisco: 415-777-1077
http://www.harlotsf.com
Plush couches, dark arts, and an attractive crowd, when there is one. Staff is known for being extremely rude to its patrons.

JOHN COLINS
138 Minna St., San Francisco: 415-512-7493
http://www.johncolins.com
No wait, no cover, and awesome tables and couches to hang out in. Chill, relaxed atmosphere with good drinks.

MR. SMITH'S
34 7th St., San Francisco: 415-355-9991
http://www.maximumproductions.com
Great place on weekends. Lounge upstairs, dance downstairs. Sketchy area but once inside, you'll be fine.

MARS BAR & RESTAURANT
798 Brannan St., San Francisco: 415-621-6277
http://www.marsbarsf.com
Three different areas to hang out. Lounge, dance floor and outdoor bar. Cheap drinks and good bar food.

MARTUNI'S
4 Valencia St., San Francisco: 415-241-0205

http://www.martunis.ypguides.net
Fun and chic ambiance in this lounge piano bar. Great martini's.

MEZZANINE
444 Jessie St., San Francisco: 415-625-8880
http://www.mezzaninesf.com
This place is hit or miss, after all, you can't please everybody all of the time. Dance club and live music venue.

THE SHOWDOWN
10 6th St., San Francisco: 415-503-0684
http://www.showdownsf.com
Chill and not super packed, this place is fun and serves a good, stiff drink.

UNION SQUARE

CANTINA
580 Sutter St., San Francisco: 415-398-0195
http://www.cantinasf.com
A good bar for many reasons. Never a cover, owners and staff are personable, good DJ's and small enough to be intimate but big enough to shake your bon-bon should you wish to do so.

THE CELLAR
685 Sutter St., San Francisco: 415-441-5678
http://www.cellarsf.com
Great place to cut loose and dance the night away. Parking will be a challenge and there is a $10 cover charge on the weekends.

HARRY DENTON'S STARLIGHT ROOM
450 Powell St., San Francisco: 415-395-8595
http://www.harrydenton.com
Dance in the evenings with a DJ and live music or brunch with the drag queens in the afternoon, which ever you decide, chances are you'll want to come back. Amazing panoramic views from every angle.

REDWOOD ROOM
The Clift Hotel
495 Geary St., San Francisco: 415-929-2372
www.clifthotel.com

Upscale bar with a 1930s speakeasy vibe. Really cool. Check out the creepy paintings on the wall, they seem to follow you around. A little on the expensive side.

RUBY SKYE
420 Mason St., San Francisco: 415-693-0777
www.rubyskye.com
Drinks aren't cheap, but they sure make them strong. Top DJ's spinning House and Trance. Top 40s and Hip Hop music is played in the smoking room on the second floor.

SLIDE
430 Mason St., San Francisco: 415-421-1916
http://www.slidesf.com
This place has good music, way more men then women, and be prepared to deal with a few weirdos. This place could also use some good ventilation.

TUNNEL TOP
601 Bush St., San Francisco: 415-722-6620
NO WEBSITE
The bar has two floors, dark, very chill, and live music. Great place to meet friends for cocktails. Friendly bartenders, cash only bar.

VESSEL
85 Campton Pl., San Francisco: 415-433-8585
http://www.vesselsf.com
The venue is okay, the dancers are cute, the drinks are normal San Francisco club prices and the crowd is very diverse.

SAN FRANCISCO GAY BARS

**THE CASTRO
LOWER HAIGHT / HAYES VALLEY
SOUTH OF MARKET (SOMA)
POLK STREET
THE MISSION**

THE CASTRO

440 CASTRO
440 Castro St., San Francisco: 415-621-8732
the440.com
Formerly Daddy's, the renaming to 440 Castro hasn't changed the clientele. Mostly men in their 30s and 40s pack this Castro neighborhood favorite located across the street from the historic Castro Theatre.

BADLANDS
4121 18th St., San Francisco: 415-626-9320
badlands-sf.com
Arguably the Castro's best dance bar, you'll often find a line on weekends, but dancing every night. Mostly men in their 20s and 30s come here to dance, enjoy the videos, and do what gay boys do best.

BLACKBIRD
2124 Market St., San Francisco: 415-503-0630
blackbirdbar.com
Blackbird takes the prize for sexy specialty drinks and cocktails in the Castro. And with a stylish, sophisticated atmosphere, it's a great spot to meet up with friends. Try their signature drink, the Blackbird Royale.

BLUSH!
476 Castro St., San Francisco: 415-558-0893
blushwinebar.com
Great Wine Bar in the heart of the Castro, Blush Wine Bar couldn't have a gayer location, right on Castro Street and steps away from all the gay action. With a fabulous wine list and comfortable atmosphere, this place is

a great way to hang with friends in a mellow atmosphere and still leave with a buzz.

BOY BAR
2369 Market St. (at Castro st.), San Francisco: 415-861-3846
guspresents.com
Wet underwear contests. Great music and everybody seems to be pretty chill. $5 cover.

CHURCHILL
198 Church St. (at Market St.), San Francisco: no phone
churchillsf.com
Busy little bar with a Winston Churchill theme, God knows why.

EDGE
4149 18th St., San Francisco: no phone
edgesf.com
This leather bar is a community favorite with a mostly 40s crowd. Nightly drink specials, $8 mason jar drinks.

HARVEY'S
500 Castro St., San Francisco: 415-431-4278
harveyssf.com
Harvey's is a bar/restaurant that is a perfect place to meet your friends and enjoy a burger. Harvey's hosts drag shows every second and fourth Saturday and a variety of other performances, including comedy and jazz on some week nights.

LAST CALL
3988 18th St., San Francisco: 415-861-1310
thelastcallbar.com
A low-key bar full of locals. Formerly known as the Men's Room, Last Call is really a local bar where the neighborhooddies hang out.

LIME
2247 Market St., San Francisco: 415-621-5256
lime-sf.com
(web site under construction at press time)
Lime is a Trendy bar/restaurant that looks as if it stepped out of an Austin Power's movie. The front lounge area is a fun place to hang, and the restaurant, which features small plates, is packed during for weekend brunch.

LOOKOUT BAR
3600 16th St., San Francisco: 415-431-0306
lookoutsf.com
Fun bar overlooking Market Street, visit this bar when the weather is nice and find a place out on the balcony to watch people go by. Crowded during happy hour, and fills up on Sunday afternoons.

MARTUNI'S
4 Valencia St., San Francisco: 415-241-0205
martunis.ypguides.net
Piano bar featuring Martini-style cocktails draws local vocalists who belt out the usual show tunes with sometimes good (and, oh dear, sometimes bad) results.

MIDNIGHT SUN
4067 18th St., San Francisco: 415-861-4186
midnightsunsf.com
(web site under construction st press time)
Best known for its funny, camp, kitsch, and music videos, Midnight Sun is a small space often crammed with its 30s male crowd. Monday is two for one drink night.

MINT
1942 Market St., San Francisco: 415-626-4726
themint.net
The Mint (named for the San Francisco Mint dominating the hill behind the bar) is the only place in San Francisco for gay Karaoke. The crowd is fun and mixed (boys and girls).

MIX
4086 18th St., San Francisco: 415-431-8616
sfmixbar.com
A dark front bar with a pool table opens up to a fab patio area in the back, which makes this bar a popular spot for smokers.

MOBY DICK
4049 18th St., San Francisco: 415-861-1199
http://www.mobydicksf.com/
A very friendly bar with mostly men in their 30s crowd, Moby's has been enjoying a resurgence in popularity, making it quite crowded and fun on the weekends.

PILSNER INN
225 Church St., San Francisco: 415-621-7058
pilsnerinn.com
The Pilsner has a pub-like atmosphere with a pool table, darts, pin ball machines, a large selection of beers, and a great patio area. The crowd is low key, mostly men in their 30s.

Q BAR
456 Castro St., San Francisco: 415-864-2877
qbarsf.com
Small Space; Big crowds. Q Bar has taken over the popular space vacated by Bar On Castro, which relocated to Church Street. The small but pulsating bar in the heart of the Castro will be renovated by day but stay open nights. Many of the special event nights, such as Jaunita More's Booty Call Wednesdays and Tuesday's women's nights remain.

THE RESIDENCE
718 14th St., San Francisco: 415-797-8866
no web site
Mixed Crowd in the Castro, the Residence is the newest bar to hit the Castro Area at the former home of Amber. The mixed crowds come back to find out where fictitious owner "Mr. Goodbar" has been on his recent travels, as they change the cultural shift of the monthly drink focus to correlate with his international adventures.

TOAD HALL
4146 18th St., San Francisco: 415-621-2811
toadhallbar.com
Badlands Redux, opened in February 2009, Toad Hall is an important addition to the Castro bar scene, its name a homage to the legendary '70s bar of the same name. The bar features a large space with a cool water feature behind the expansive bar. The covered outdoor patio in back is basically an end-run on the city's ban on smoking in public venues, much like the patio at the Mix bar just down the street. Under the same ownership as Badlands, directly across 18th Street, the bar has the same cookie-cutter design, and features a similarly young, tight-jeans and T-shirt crowd. Badlands is hugely successful, so the strategy makes a certain sense but as such doesn't really offer a new bar experience. In fact, on a busy weekend night streams of boys can be seen jaywalking from Badlands to Toad Hall, and back again. The scenario is not without its benefits,

however: Faster service and fewer lines to get drinks at the bar can now be expected.

TRIGGER
2344 Market St., San Francisco: 415-551-CLUB
clubtrigger.com
Web site was down at press time
New York style comes to San Francisco, Trigger is as swanky-cool as they come, especially in San Francisco. It's New York downtown posh come to bohemian San Francisco, and there are many stylin' gay men and lesbians who will appreciate that appeal. The expensive cocktails may dampen their enthusiasm a bit.

TWIN PEAKS
401 Castro St., San Francisco: 415-864-9470
twinpeakstavern.com
The long-established Twin Peaks is an icon in San Francisco gay bar history. The bartenders and crowd remember way back when, and after a few drinks will start telling you all about it. Crowd is usually 50s and older, but a fun bar in which to be introduced to the history of the Castro.

LOWER HAIGHT / HAYES VALLEY

UNDERGROUND SF
424 Haight St. (bet. Webster & Fillmore Sts.), San Francisco: 415-864-7386
NO WEBSITE
Gay dive bar with dance floor and small patio in back. Sometimes go-go boys mount the bar for some show-off fun. It can get very crowded, but the hip crowd is sexy and frisky. Saturdays are the most packed--and the gayest.

SOUTH OF MARKET (SOMA)

THE CRIB
715 Harrison St. (at 3rd), San Francisco: 415-546-7938
thecribsf.com

On Thursdays, gay & lesbian dance night for the 18+ crowd. The Crib is San Francisco's only long-running club that caters to the 18 & over crowd. The weekly happening is wildly popular.

ENDUP
401 6th St. (bet. Harrison St. & James Lick Fwy.), San Francisco: 415-646-0999
theendup.com
Web site down at press time)
As its name suggests, the Endup is often the last stop for gay clubbing in San Francisco. Fridays are the best night of the week for dancing gay boys and partiers.

HOLE IN THE WALL
1369 Folson St., San Francisco: 415-431-4695
holeinthewallsaloon.com
A leather/biker bar with a rougher crowd for cruising, the Hole is true to its name with mostly men in their 30s and 40s.

HOLY COW
1535 Folsom St., San Francisco: 415-621-6087
theholycow.com
Home of Honey Sundays, the Holy Cow tends straight, but Sundays it's gay gay gay! Check out the Honey Scene and get in one of the best weeklies in San Francisco.

KOK BAR SF
1225 Folsom St., San Francisco: 415-255-2427
kokbarsf.com
SOMA leather bar. OK BAR is a new addition to the SOMA leather and gear bar scene, formerly dubbed Chaps 2. According to the the web site: "Its not just leather, but leather is a very big part of our bar." KOK BAR is the latest incarnation of an iconic SF bar. Chuck Slaton and Ron Morrison signed a lease for 375 11th Street (the current DNA Lounge) in 1981 and turned the auto body shop into one of SOMAs infamous leather bars before it eventually went out of business during the AIDS crisis.

LONE STAR SALOON
1354 Harrison St., San Francisco: 415-863-9999
lonestarsaloon.com
Billing itself as the world's first bear bar, the Lone Star has a patio area that attracts a leather daddy crowd.

POWERHOUSE
1357 Folsom St., San Francisco: 415-552-8689
powerhouse-sf.com
A very cruisy leather bar with a back room and a patio, the Powerhouse is a leather bar for those looking for some action.

RAVEN BAR
1151 Folsom St. (bet. 7th & 8th Sts.), San Francisco: 415-431-1151
www.ravenbarsf.com/
Dark lightning, leather booths and antique furnishings are meant to evoke "film noir," and if this is what you want to think, OK. It's just a gussied up gay bar with fancy (expensive) cocktails.

THE STUD
399 Ninth St. (bet. Harrison & Sheridan), San Francisco: 415-863-6623
studsf.com
The Stud is a fun queer bar with theme nights that include Trannyshack Tuesdays and Planet Big (for big men and their admirers) on the Second and Fourth Fridays.

POLK STREET

AUNT CHARLIE'S
133 Turk St. (at Taylor), San Francisco: 415-441-2922
auntcharlieslounge.com
The Original Drag Bar, Aunt Charlies is a local and traveler favorite, and a second home to the transgender community who have supported it for years. With Events Wednesday through Saturday including The Hot Boxxx Girls, The TubeSteak Connection, and the Dream Queens Review, there is never a dull moment.

THE CINCH
1723 Polk St. (bet. Clay & Washington), San Francisco: 415-776-4162
thecinch.com
This western bar is complete with saloon doors. Also, don't miss the refrigerator door entrance to the men's room, hilarious. The Cinch is frequented by a friendly 30s something mixed crowd.

DECO LOUNGE
510 Larkin St. (bet. Turk & Eddy), San Francisco: 415-346-2025

decosf.com
Deco Lounge features a variety of theme nights.

DIVA'S
1081 Post St. (bet. Polk & Larkin), San Francisco: 415-474-3482
www.divassf.com
Diva's drag, dance bar and nightclub is transgender friendly. It has a $10 cover, which is kind of steep for the neighborhood.

GANGWAY
841 Larkin St. (bet. Geary & Myrtle), San Francisco: 415-776-6828
NO WEBSITE
The Oldest Gay Bar in San Francisco, The Gangway may have seen better days, as ABC laws have cracked down on a lot of the events that transpire there. However, for a chill time at a sleepy old bar, this place gives you a chance to see some history—namely dive bar history and stories from drunks that just can't be replicated.

THE MISSION

EL RIO
3158-A Mission St. (bet. Powers & Precita), San Francisco: 415- 282-3325
elriosf.com
A mixed crowd pleases all tastes, though not strictly a gay bar, El Rio always has a nice gay contingency mixing and mingling through the often very crowded space. A welcoming and unpretentious option for a night out.

ESTA NOCHE
3079 16th St. (bet. Caledonia & Rondel), San Francisco: 415-861-5757
estanocheclub.com
Latino's meet drag queens at San Francisco's Latin gay bar. Esta Noche is located in a sketchy neighborhood so come with friends or go on a Sunday afternoon if it's your first time there.

THE LEXINGTON CLUB
3464 19th St. (bet. Lexington & Valencia), San Francisco: 415-863-2052
lexingtonclub.com
A lesbian beer bar on a quiet street in the Mission, the crowd is mostly women in their 20s and 30s.

THEE PARKSIDE
1600 17th St., San Francisco: 415-252-1330
theeparkside.com
Alternative hangout off the beaten path, here you can get away from the glitter of the Castro at this old-school lesbian favorite. Stiff drinks with live music and a punk rock mentality make this a great place to find a more culturally nuanced gay crowd.

THE PHONE BOOTH
1398 S. Van Ness Ave. (bet. 24th & 25th), San Francisco: 415-648-4683
NO WEBSITE
Mixed crowds at this local hangout, The Phonebooth is favored by a Mission District scenester crowd, but has managed to not be defined by the hipster movement. It is a great dive to just go grab a drink at with friends and run into your favorite locals.

STRAY BAR
309 Cortland Ave. (bet. Bocana & Bennington), San Francisco: 415-821-9263
straybarsf.com
Sit. Stay. Drink. Nestled up in Bernal Heights, Stray Bar caters to the neighborhood by welcoming canine friends inside (assuming they have a human companion). The crowd is low key, and leans more towards the ladies.

TRUCK
1900 Folsom St., San Francisco: 415-252-0306
trucksf.com
Truck is located between SOMA and the Mission. It's a small neighborhood bar with a pool table and not-great bar food (think burgers and garlic fries). Still it has garnered a consistent following since it opened.

WILD SIDE WEST
424 Cortland Ave. (bet. Bennington & Wool), San Francisco: 415-647-3099
www.wildwestside.com
Neighborhood lesbian bar with garden in the back. Mingle with the girls around a fabulous old bar and pool table that sits in the middle of the small, cozy place. On a nice evening share a drink in the garden patio.

Chapter 5
ATTRACTIONS

ABOVE THE WINE COUNTRY BALLOONS AND TOURS
397 Aviation Boulevard, Santa Rosa: 707-538-7359
http://www.balloontours.com
Celebrating 35 years with the highest Five-Star Rated, FAA-PUC Certified Service, view the redwoods, Russian River, majestic mountains, the Pacific Coast, San Francisco skyline and lush vineyards. Free champagne brunch, choose from a full menu, hosted by the pilot. Private flights for two or larger groups.

ALCATRAZ CRUISES
Pier 33, Alcatraz Landing, San Francisco: 415-981-ROCK (7625)
http://www.alcatrazcruises.com
The official (and only) transportation carrier to Alcatraz Island. Guaranteed lowest prices. Advance reservations recommended. Book tours and print tickets on-line to avoid the crowds.
Alcatraz and history go hand in hand. Once home to some of America's most notorious criminals, the federal penitentiary that operated here from 1934 to 1963 brought a dark mystique to the Rock. The presence of infamous inmates like Al "Scarface" Capone, and the "Birdman" Robert Stroud helped to establish the island's notoriety. To this day, Alcatraz is best known as one of the world's most legendary prisons.

ALL ABOUT CHINATOWN WALKING TOURS
P.O. Box 640145, San Francisco: 415-982-8839
http://www.allaboutchinatown.com
Join a fun-filled, behind-the-scenes tour of colorful Chinatown with insider and native, Linda Lee. Unique tour covers history, culture, traditions, and food. Finish with a gourmet dim sum luncheon. Recommended by National Geographic Traveler.

AQUARIUM OF THE BAY
Pier 39, on the Embarcadero at Beach Street, San Francisco: 415-623-5300
http://www.aquariumofthebay.org
Visit San Francisco's only waterfront aquarium. Meet 20,000 amazing marine animals as you walk through 300 feet of crystal clear tunnels. Touch

sharks and rays. Open daily except Dec. 25. Summer hours 9am-8pm. Most other times M-Th 10am-6pm, F-Su until 7pm. Admission $16.95 adults; $8 seniors (age 65+) and children (ages 3-11); $39.95 family (2 adults, 2 children). Children under 3 free. Prices and hours subject to change.

BAY AREA DISCOVERY MUSEUM
Fort Baker 557 McReynolds Road, Sausalito: 415-339-3900
http://www.baykidsmuseum.org
A one-of-a-kind indoor/outdoor children's museum located under the Golden Gate Bridge dedicated to nurturing creativity through hands-on arts, science and cultural exhibitions.

BEACH BLANKET BABYLON
678 Beach Blanket Babylon Boulevard (Green Street), San Francisco: 415-421-4222
http://beachblanketbabylon.com
Steve Silver's Beach Blanket Babylon, the longest running musical revue in theatre history, is a zany musical spoof of pop culture with extravagant costumes and outrageously huge hats. With sold-out performances since 1974, Beach Blanket Babylon is an internationally acclaimed San Francisco institution. With more than 12,000 performances in San Francisco, the show has performed for standing room only during its London and Las Vegas engagements. Beach Blanket Babylon continually evolves in its hilarious parodies of current events and popular icons as today's headlines unfold.

CHARLES M. SCHULZ MUSEUM
2301 Hardies Lane, Santa Rosa: 707-579-4452
http://www.schulzmuseum.org
Dedicated to preserving the legacy of Peanuts creator, Charles M. Schulz, this museum offers exhibits of original art, entertaining programs and tours. Group tours and use of research library by appointment only.

BEAU WINE TOURS
21707 Eighth Street East, Sonoma: 707-938-8001
http://www.beauwinetours.com
 Napa Wine Tours and Sonoma Wine Tours, by Beau Wine Tours & Limousine Service, are the perfect solution for a great wine tasting day in California's Napa Valley or Sonoma County. Enjoy the company of a knowledgeable local wine tour guide at the wheel, sit back and relax, and

take advantage of the most elegant and safest method to enjoy our outstanding Napa wine tours or Sonoma Wine Tours.

BOUDIN AT THE WHARF
160 Jefferson Street, San Francisco: 415-928-1849
http://www.boudinbakery.com
Set in the heart of Fisherman's Wharf, two-story flagship building allows visitors to observe the bakery in action. Learn how sourdough French bread is made and why it cannot be baked anywhere else on earth. Free trip to tasting room included with Museum & Bakery tour.

THE CASTRO
www.castrosf.org
The Castro District, commonly referenced as The Castro, is a neighborhood in Eureka Valley in San Francisco, California. The Castro is one of America's first and best-known gay neighborhoods, and it is currently its largest. Having transformed from a working-class neighborhood through the 1960s and 1970s, the Castro remains a symbol and source of lesbian, gay, bisexual, and transgender (LGBT) activism and events.

San Francisco's gay village is mostly concentrated in the business district that is located on Castro Street from Market Street to 19th Street. It extends down Market Street toward Church Street and on both sides of the Castro neighborhood from Church Street to Eureka Street.

There's also a great walking tour, **CRUISIN' THE CASTRO**, that takes you on a walking tour that gives you an interesting historical perspective on the city's famous gay quarter. Runs 2 hours from 10 a.m. to noon Tuesday-Saturday. 415-255-1821. www.cruisinthecastro.com.

CASTRO THEATRE
429 Castro St., San Francisco: 415-621-6120.
www.castrotheatre.com
This grand cinemas palace went up in 1922, so it saw a lot of silent features before talkies took over. (There's still a working organ sometime played before movies.) This is really a marvel, and ought to be seen, especially if you've never been in one of these grand old movie houses.

CHINATOWN
Walking Tour: 650-355-9657 / www.wokwiz.com

The entrance to Chinatown at Grant Avenue and Bush Street is called the "Dragon's Gate." Inside are 24 blocks of hustle and bustle, most of it taking place along Grant Avenue, the oldest street in San Francisco. This city within a city is best explored on foot; exotic shops, renowned restaurants, food markets, temples and small museums comprise its boundaries. Visitors can buy ancient potions from herb shops, relax and enjoy a "dim sum" lunch or witness the making of fortune cookies.

CONTEMPORARY JEWISH MUSEUM
736 Mission St., San Francisco: 415-655-7800
http://www.thecjm.org
Located in downtown San Francisco, the Contemporary Jewish Museum presents dynamic exhibitions and educational programs, exploring contemporary perspectives on Jewish culture, history and ideas.

FISHERMAN'S WHARF
http://www.fishermanswharf.org/
http://visitfishermanswharf.com/
Fisherman's Wharf is also home to Pier 39, a festive waterfront marketplace that is one of the city's most popular attractions. A community of California sea lions has taken up residence on the floats to the west of the pier and visitors line the nearby railing to watch their antics. From there it's a short walk to the Wax Museum, Ripley's Believe It or Not! And the famous crab vendors selling walk-away crab and shrimp cocktails.

FERRY PLAZA FARMERS MARKET
1 Ferry Building, San Francisco: 415-983-8030
http://www.ferrybuildingmarketplace.com
The Ferry Plaza Farmers Market is a California certified farmers market operated by the nonprofit Center for Urban Education about Sustainable Agriculture (CUESA). The market is widely acclaimed for both the quality and diversity of its fresh farm products, and artisan and prepared foods. It is renowned throughout the country as one of the top farmers markets to visit. On any day, especially Saturdays, some of San Francisco's best known chefs, and most famous farmers, can be seen at the market. The market provides a forum for people to learn about food and agriculture. Each week nearly 25,000 shoppers visit the farmers market.
The farmers market is open three days a week—Tuesdays, Thursdays and Saturdays. On Tuesdays and Thursdays, the smaller markets occupy the front of the building along the Embarcadero; on Saturdays, the much larger market is held both in front of the Ferry Building and on the rear plaza overlooking the Bay. The markets offer fruits, vegetables, herbs, flowers,

meats and eggs from small regional farmers and ranchers, many of whom are certified organic. A wealth of other products include regional artisan specialties such as breads, cheeses and jams. The Thursday market features an array of artisan street food: wood-fired pizza, grilled meats, sandwiches, and tacos, while the Saturday market also includes local restaurants serving a variety of hot, delicious meals.

CUESA conducts a wide variety of educational programs, including in-market talks and cooking demonstrations, farm tours, cooking classes, and panel discussions. They also produce fact sheets, teacher resources, a free weekly eletter and a comprehensive website.

GHIRARDELLI SQUARE
http://ghirardellisquare.com
When you think of Ghirardelli your first thought may be of chocolate. However, Ghirardelli Square isn't just about chocolate, it's about history, tradition and enjoyment. Ghirardelli Square translates into "a fun destination with a vibrant atmosphere". Ghirardelli Square restaurants offer something for everyone. You can enjoy a wine tasting experience, fine dining or take the kids to the Ice Cream and Chocolate Shop, there's options galore at the all new Ghirardelli Square.

Today, Ghirardelli Square is a unique San Francisco destination that includes a mix of upscale shopping, fine dining, wine bars, spa facilities and live entertainment. Ghirardelli Square also represents one of the city's newest options for luxury living. Fairmont Heritage Place, a new development offering luxury residences is located at the square.

Ghirardelli Square is a historic San Francisco landmark, located on the beautiful San Francisco bay just a block from the cable car turnaround on the west side of Fisherman's Wharf.

GOLDEN GATE BRIDGE
The Golden Gate Bridge, the most famous bridge in the world, manages to impress even the most experienced travelers with its stunning 1.7-mile span. Approximately 120,000 automobiles drive across it every day. A pedestrian walkway also allows the crossing on foot, and bikes are allowed on the western side. The Golden Gate Bridge is said to be one of the most photographed things on Earth.

GOLDEN GATE BRIDGE
goldengatebridge.org / 415-455-2000
Has a Visitors' Center at Bridge Plaza on the southeast end of the bridge. The Golden Gate Bridge, the most famous bridge in the world, manages to impress even the most experienced travelers with its stunning 1.7-mile

span. Over 100,000 automobiles drive across it every day. A pedestrian walkway also allows the crossing on foot, and bikes are allowed on the western side. The Golden Gate Bridge is said to be one of the most photographed things on Earth. The Bridge turned 75 in 2012, and as of that date, there had been 1,400 suicides from it, 3 births took place there, and all sorts of other things have happened there.

GOLDEN GATE FORTUNE COOKIE FACTORY
56 Ross Alley, San Francisco: 415-781-3956
As you walk down Ross Alley, you may just pass this fortune cookie factory, but the aroma of the freshly made fortune cookies will draw you in. This factory has been supplying fortune cookies to Chinatown and around the world since 1962.
You can bring in your own fortunes, make custom cookies great for dinner parties at around $6 for 50 cookies a cheap way to impress your friends.

GOLDEN GATE FERRY
Golden Gate Ferry Terminal, Market and Embarcadero Behind the Ferry Building, San Francisco: 415-455-2000
http://www.goldengate.org
Ferries depart frequently from behind the south end of the Ferry Building to Sausalito and Larkspur in Marin County. Services include half-hour crossings to Sausalito and 30- or 45-minute crossings to Larkspur.

GRAY LINE
415-434-8687
http://www.sanfranciscosightseeing.com
Explore this most culturally diverse and beautiful of cities. Your guided journey will highlight famous landmarks and familiarize you with the unique sociology of San Francisco.
Narrative includes Victorian houses, Civic Center, Union Square, Nob Hill, Cable Cars, Chinatown, North Beach, Coit Tower, Fisherman's Wharf, Marina District, Palace of Fine Arts, The Presidio, Golden Gate Park, Twin Peaks, Golden Gate Bridge and more.
Scheduled stops include Vista Point at the Golden Gate Bridge, the panoramic view of the city from atop Twin Peaks and other photo opportunities recommended by your guide. From past to present and hills to shiny sea, your experience will be most memorable. Seating is first come first serve. Tour lasts 3 and 1/2 hours. About $50.

HAIGHT ASHBURY FLOWER POWER WALKING TOUR
P.O. Box 170106, San Francisco: 415-863-1621

http://www.haightashburytour.com
The Haight Ashbury Flower Power Walking Tour is your backstage pass to the coolest area in the universe. Stroll through the cosmic history of it all, from rock'n roll to art, fashion and architecture, this fantastic walking adventure gives you a real insight into the cosmic draw of the Haight-Ashbury. The tour is approximately 60% hippy history and 40% general neighborhood history and architecture, but it's always 100% 'far-out' fun. Saunter along the same streets that Janis Joplin, Jimi Hendrix, The Grateful Dead, Joni Mitchell and countless others etched their marks into the collective alternative culture and creativity of the 20th century.

HANGAR ONE VODKA DISTILLERY
2601 Monarch St., Alameda: 510-864-0635
http://www.hangarone.com
Established in 1982, offers people a chance to taste their hand-crafted spirits while enjoying breathtaking views of San Francisco. W-Sa noon-7pm, Su noon-6pm. $10 fee for full tastings. 21 and over. Tours of the distillery every Saturday at 1pm. Group rates available for private tour and tasting. Minimum number in a group 15.

LOMBARD STREET
Between Hyde and Leavenworth Streets
Often billed as the "crookedest street," San Francisco's Lombard Street is, in fact, neither the crookedest nor the steepest street in the city, let alone the world. Oddly, that fact doesn't deter the hordes of tourists who come every year to see this famous street, built with eight switchbacks on a 40-degree slope.
The main attraction of Lombard Street is watching people drive down the crooked, one-block section, or driving down it yourself. On a busy day, a seemingly-endless stream of automobiles and scooters buzz down, their passengers squealing in mock fear at every turn. If you're on foot, you can walk down (or up) the sidewalks and watch the show.
The best place to photograph Lombard Street is from the bottom, looking up.
The "crooked" section of Lombard is between Hyde and Leavenworth, just a few blocks above Ghirardelli Square.
The Powell-Hyde cable car stops at the top of Lombard Street. You can also get there by walking up Hyde (very steep) from Ghirardelli Square, up Leavenworth (one block east, less steep) or by walking west from North Beach on Lombard Street, but the best way to get here depends on where you're coming from. Best Time to Visit: The flowers are nicest in spring and summer, and morning is the best time for photographs.

MARRAKECH MAGIC THEATER
419 O'Farrell Street, San Francisco:
http://www.sanfranciscomagictheater.com
An amazing one-of-a-kind interactive show in an intimate setting. Magician Peter Morrison will charm with elegant magic and dazzle with mentalism. F at 8:30pm, Su at 6:30pm. $38 for Fridays, $35 adults, $20 children (5-12) for Sundays.
Have an experience to last a lifetime. At The Marrakech Magic Theater, cherished memories are made during Peter Morrison's unique two-hour comedy and magic experience. The evening begins with drinks, appetizers, and pre-show entertainment in the Sultan's Oasis lounge, and ends with Peter's unforgettable 75 minute performance in the Main Showroom. The Main Showroom is an intimate close-up theater, perfect for high spirits and Peter's extraordinary performances. You'll witness intriguing feats of mentalism, sleight of hand miracles, and throughout, his clean comedy will keep you laughing.

NAPA VALLEY WINE TRAIN
1275 McKinstry Street, Napa: 707-253-2111
http://winetrain.com
A leisurely three-hour, 36-mile journey takes passengers through the heart of the wine country. The train boasts opulently restored vintage lounge cars and a 1916 Pullman converted into a kitchen complete with a stainless steel gallery and a window wall allowing chefs to be viewed in action. Lunch or dinner served in richly appointed dining cars. For families with young children; an inexpensive a la carte menu available. Some runs make a stop at a winery; private winery tours and murder mystery dinners are often scheduled. Daily excursions, schedule varies. Admission $49.50-$184. Advance reservations suggested.

NORTH BEACH
North Beach, the city's Italian quarter, isn't a beach at all. It's a neighborhood of romantic European-style sidewalk cafes, restaurants and shops centered near Washington Square along Columbus and Grant avenues. The beautiful Church of Saints Peter and Paul is a beloved landmark. Coit Tower atop Telegraph Hill offers a splendid vantage point for photos of the bridges and the Bay. Inside the tower, floor-to-ceiling murals painted in the 1930s depict scenes of early San Francisco.

OPEN TOP SIGHTSEEING SAN FRANCISCO
99 Jefferson Street, San Francisco: 415-850-9524

http://www.opentopsightseeing.com
Enjoy a spectacular one- and-a-half-hour tour on a new open top double-decker tour bus 20 stops, hop on and off as much as you like. Scheduled daily departures 9am-5pm. Adult $35, $18 child 5-12, free child 4 and under.

PIER 39
Beach Street & The Embarcadero, San Francisco
http://www.pier39.com
PIER 39 is located on the northernmost point of the San Francisco peninsula providing visitors with postcard views of Alcatraz, the Golden Gate and Bay Bridges, the San Francisco Bay and the City skyline. Telescopes are placed along the location's perimeter road for viewing the sights. PIER 39 is the "Best Place to People Watch (San Francisco)" as voted by the San Francisco Chronicle's Readers' Choice competition.

RIDE THE DUCKS SAN FRANCISCO - SAN FRANCISCO DUCK TOURS
2766 Taylor St., San Francisco: 415-596-9929
http://www.sanfranciscoducks.com
A Ride The Ducks San Francisco tour includes an exciting ride on a "land and water" duck boat. It looks pretty dorky and even stupid as it bounces around town, but it's actually quite a bit of fun. Ride through the historic streets and neighborhoods of San Francisco. Splash down and cruise famous McCovey Cove. Drive the duck, if you want. Quack along with the captain and the music aboard this 90-minute city adventure. Your entertaining captain mixes fun, music, and history into an interactive experience better than any other San Francisco tour.

SAN FRANCISCO CABLE CAR MUSEUM
1201 Mason Street, San Francisco: 415-474-1887
http://www.cablecarmuseum.org/
The one-of-a-kind San Francisco Cable Car Museum deserves special attention. In the historic Cable Car Barn & Powerhouse, the site where the cable system has operated since 1907, visitors can view the actual cable winding machinery as it reels 11 miles of steel at a steady pace of nine-and-a-half miles per hour. Antique cable cars are also on display, including the first one dating from 1873. Always free. It only takes $5 to ride a cable car, the only moving national historic landmark in America, to the museum via the Powell-Hyde or Powell-Mason lines.

SAN FRANCISCO GIANTS
AT&T Park 24 Willie Mays Plaza, San Francisco: 415-972-2000

http://www.sfgiants.com
AT&T Park is home to the San Francisco Giants. Located on the City's scenic waterfront, the ballpark is a short walk from downtown San Francisco and Moscone Center and is accessible by every means of public transit.

SAN FRANCISCO ZOO
Sloat Blvd. & Great Highway, San Francisco: 415-753-7080
http://www.sfzoo.org
The San Francisco Zoo is Northern California's largest zoological park with more than 225 species of animals in naturalistic settings. Highlights include the African Savanna, Lemur Forest, Meerkats and Prairie Dogs, the Feline Conservation Center, Otter River, Eagle Island, Gorilla World, Penguin Island, Sumatran tigers, African wart hog exhibit and Koala Crossing. The Children's Zoo gives young folks the thrill of feeding and petting their favorite barnyard animals, and if little legs are starting to weary, the Little Puffer Zoo Train ($4) makes regular circuits of the grounds.

ST. PATRICK'S CATHOLIC CHURCH
756 Mission Street, San Francisco: 415-421-3730
http://www.spcsf.org
St. Patrick's is uniquely a sign of God's loving presence. It was here when the miners left for the gold country, it served the Irish immigrants, withstood the great fire and earthquake of 1906, continued to serve the Irish, then the Spanish-speaking, now the Filipino community, the numerous tourists and conventioneers and always the business world by which it is surrounded. Unchanged in the midst of change, it still repeats for all the message of Him who is the resurrection and the life.
St. Patrick Church's elegant architecture is accented by the Irish national colors, green Connemara marble, and white and gold Botticino marble. Each of the patron saints of the thirty-two counties of Ireland is proudly showcased on the Tiffany-style stained-glass windows, which also depict the rich heritage and traditions of the Irish.

UNION SQUARE
http://www.unionsquareshop.com/
Union Square is the place for serious shoppers. Major departments stores and the most exclusive designer boutiques line streets like Post, Sutter, Geary, Grant, Stockton and Powell. The Westfield San Francisco Shopping Centre houses the largest Bloomingdale's outside of New York and the second largest Nordstrom in the U.S.

VICTORIAN HOME HISTORICAL WALKING TOUR
Corner Powell & Post, at Union Square: 415-252-9485
www.victorianwalk.com
You can't really get San Francisco until you see some of the great houses that dot the city. Tour runs 2.5 hours, is fun and not too fast paced.

YOSEMITE TOURS
Extranomical Adventures, Inc.
501 Bay St., San Francisco: 415-357-0700
http://www.extranomical.com
The 1 day Yosemite & Giant Sequoias tour from San Francisco is an excellent way to get the most out of your Yosemite Tour. Yosemite National Park tours maximizes the time you spend in Yosemite National Park by starting early and traveling more efficiently in a 15 Passenger Van or mini-bus. This allows time to cover the Yosemite Valley & the Giant Sequoias in one day and spend more time in the park (at least 5 hours) than any other one day Yosemite tour available. They also offer 2, 3, & 5 day overnight tours to Yosemite from San Francisco with private hotel room or shared dorm room accommodation available. Regardless of your preference our wide array of Yosemite Tours and lodging options will surely meet your needs. $139

Chapter 6
SHOPPING

CHESTNUT STREET SHOPPING
Chestnut and Scott Streets: San Francisco
www.chestnutshop.com/

Chestnut is a street lined with a mix of sophisticated shops, beauty outlets and restaurants alongside brand name retailers. While unique and offbeat in nature, Chestnut Street retains a distinctive neighborhood feel. Here shoppers and locals find incredible shoe boutiques like Rabat featuring trendy but functional footwear and specialty shops like Blue Bird, a gift shop carrying kitschy gifts like porcelain dolls and oversized potato heads. Well-known retailers, like Gap Body or the small, unique Chadwick's of London for cotton and lace lingerie, lend a mass appeal. Williams-Sonoma, a neighborhood fixture, has the best in cookware, utensils and cookbooks. For beauty care, Bare Essentials or the Body Shop will keep you looking great with the best in cosmetics and skincare. A lunch break on Chestnut means a choice of Cafe Marimba, an open, airy colorful Mexican restaurant or Cozmo's which prepares wood oven meats and seafood paired with California wines. On any day, Chestnut Street is bustling with shoppers, professionals meeting for coffee at Bechelli's or neighborhood Moms with strollers shopping at Books, Inc. The highlights of this cozy San Francisco neighborhood are a sophisticated ambience and streamlined energy conducive to shopping.

BOOKS, INC.
2251 Chestnut St., San Francisco: 415-931-3633
http://www.booksinc.net
Book Store

CHADWICK'S OF LONDON
2068 Chestnut St., San Francisco: 415-775-3423
www.chadwicksoflondon.com
Elegant cotton and lace lingerie.

PAPYRUS
2275 Chestnut St., San Francisco: 415-929-0725
www.papyrusonline.com
Cards - Stationery - Wrapping - Gifts

SUN SHADE OPTIQUE
2128 Chestnut St., San Francisco: 415-749-0383
Eyewear and opticians.

CHINATOWN SHOPPING
Bush St. and Grand Ave: San Francisco
www.sanfranciscochinatown.com/

Yes, this is the largest "Chinatown" outside of China. They aren't kidding. Enter the Dragon Gates for access to another, redder and more-bustling world of shopping in San Francisco's Chinatown, tucked loudly away between North Beach and Union Square shopping. Ornate lampposts, pagoda roofs and a Bank of America that could just as well be in Shanghai highlight San Francisco's eclectic Chinatown. At every turn, candles burn and vivid silks grace the jam-packed window fronts, where import vendors sell nearly everything, including (but by no means limited to) carved Buddhas, paper parasols and regal mahogany furniture, perfect for exotic gifts or indulgent tourist fodder. Apothecaries abound, selling delicate green teas, rose-scented black teas and a variety of other ailment-banishing brews by the ounce. For a sweet surprise, the fragrant Fortune Cookie Factory tucked away on Ross Alley is an exciting find. Chinese food is just as abundant: for some of the best in San Francisco, the inexpensive House of Nanking is just off Chinatown's main drag a few blocks west on Kearny (at Jackson).

CANTON BAZAAR
616 Grant Ave., San Francisco: 415-362-5750
www.cantonbazaar.com
An array of Buddhas, hand-carved dragons, porcelain sake sets and kimonos.

CHINA STATION
456-460 Grant Ave., San Francisco: 415-397-4848

Cheap souvenirs, such as yin and yang Chinese exercise balls, kimonos, decorative fans and Buddha statues, as well as other Chinese arts and crafts.

THE WOK SHOP
718 Grant Ave., San Francisco: 415-989-3797
www.wokshop.com
No-nonsense cooking-equipment market sells woks, tea sets and more.

EMBARCADERO CENTER 1-4 SHOPPING
Sacramento to Clay Streets: San Francisco
www.**embarcaderocenter**.com/

Embarcadero is an underutilized shopping expanse, usually crowded with professionals who work in the nearby towers or locals who know this San Francisco mall is light on foot traffic but heavy on great stores and accessory shops. Embarcadero is retail haven with brand names like Gap, Banana Republic, Ann Taylor, Liz Claiborne, Victoria Secret and Express Jeans. Even though the Embarcadero holds big names, this San Francisco shopping mall has unusual stores: the Discovery Channel Store for science lovers and the Giants Dugout for the sports enthusiast. The mall's spacious outdoor and indoor design lends itself to a more comfortable and easy shopping experience. The Embarcadero is contoured for the busy shopper with wide walkways and well-placed stairwells. During sunny days, the upstairs patio is perfect for patrons dining at Fuzio, a high-energy Italian restaurant or for coffee drinkers at Java City. The shopping mall is also home to the Embarcadero Theater, a movie house showing the brightest alternative and independent films by top directors.

AMBASSADOR TOYS
2 Embarcadero Ctr. lobby, San Francisco: 415-345- 8697
www.ambassadortoys.com
Wide selection of toys, art supplies, and educational products from around the world.

FERRY BUILDING MARKETPLACE
1 Ferry Building, San Francisco: 415-983-8030
www.ferrybuildingmarketplace.com
Here you'll find one of the most interesting shopping/eating experiences in the whole city. Don't come here unless you're hungry, because you'll want to wander in and out of all the shops and eateries sampling everything.

Acme Breads, the Slanted Door (a famous Vietnamese restaurant), Hog Island Oysters and dozens of other places you'll find enticing.

The **Farmers' Market** is widely acclaimed for both the quality and diversity of its fresh farm products, and artisan and prepared foods. It is renowned throughout the country as one of the top farmers markets to visit. On any day, especially Saturdays, some of San Francisco's best known chefs, and most famous farmers, can be seen at the market. The market provides a forum for people to learn about food and agriculture. Each week nearly 25,000 shoppers visit the farmers market.

The farmers market is open three days a week—Tuesdays, Thursdays and Saturdays. On Tuesdays and Thursdays, the smaller markets occupy the front of the building along the Embarcadero; on Saturdays, the much larger market is held both in front of the Ferry Building and on the rear plaza overlooking the Bay. The markets offer fruits, vegetables, herbs, flowers, meats and eggs from small regional farmers and ranchers, many of whom are certified organic. A wealth of other products include regional artisan specialties such as breads, cheeses and jams. The Thursday market features an array of artisan street food: wood-fired pizza, grilled meats, sandwiches, and tacos, while the Saturday market also includes local restaurants serving a variety of hot, delicious meals.

CUESA conducts a wide variety of educational programs, including in-market talks and cooking demonstrations, farm tours, cooking classes, and panel discussions.

PURE BEAUTY
4 Embarcadero Ctr., street, San Francisco: 415-982-5599
www.purebeauty.com
Wide variety of professional beauty products and salon services for hair and skin.

SIKARA JEWELRY
2 Embarcadero Ctr., San Francisco: 415-434-4646
www.sikarajewelry.com
Fine Jewelry.

SEE'S CANDIES
3 Embarcadero Ctr., San Francisco: 415-391-1622
www.sees.com
World famous chocolatier.

FILLMORE STREET SHOPPING
Fillmore and California Streets: San Francisco
www.fillmoreshop.com
www.fillmorestreetsf.com/

On Fillmore Street, it's easy to feel pampered with several well-known beauty retailers and ritzy interior design boutiques fresh out of New York. Rachel Ashwell's Shabbychic furniture and bedroom design store is next to Betsy Johnson's runway shop on this luxe stretch of Fillmore that combines a busy wealthy Victorian neighborhood with a thriving San Francisco shopping center. Every shopping wish list is checked off here with select perfumeries, furniture designers like Zinc Details and specialty beauty outlets like Aveda. For shopping fuel, Fillmore street offers a Starbuck's as well as a locals-frequented Royal Grounds. A distinctly picturesque part of town, Fillmore Street maintains an air of charm and simplicity while still offering a luxurious and high-end lifestyle.

BROWSER BOOKS
2225 Fillmore St., San Francisco: 415-567-8027
http://browserbooks.indiebound.com
Interesting and hard to find books.

LINCO & CO
1908 Fillmore St., San Francisco: 415-931-8228
http://www.lincoandco.com
Fine Jewelry.

SMITH & HAWKEN
2040 Fillmore St., San Francisco: 415-776-3424
http://www.smithandhawken.com
Garden inspired products for the home.

HAIGHT STREET SHOPPING
Haight St. and Ashbury: San Francisco
www.**haight**shop.com/
www.**haightstreet**.com/

The stretch of shops, referred to by San Francisco locals as the Upper Haight, was the center of '60s psychedelia. Despite gentrification and the proliferation of stores like Ben & Jerry's and The Gap, it still retains its hippie counterculture credentials, and is dotted with Victorian houses, anarchist bookstores, piercing salons and funky clothing shops. Taking cues from New York and Los Angeles, as well as showcasing local Bay Area designers, the thoroughly modern Jaxx is a true urban outfitter, while just across the street at X-Generation, knock-offs of the originals go for much less. On Haight Street, one of the most eclectic and perennially busy San Francisco shopping stretches, San Francisco shoppers can find just about anything, from hardware to punk gear and fishnets to upscale vintage. With food and booze choices just as prolific (try Cha Cha Cha's for *sangria* and *tapas* or Kanzaman for a vanilla hookah and a beer), locals as well as out-of-towners spend time shopping (or just window gazing) on the Haight's incense-scented sidewalks. For music-philes, the bowling alley turned record store, Amoeba Records, is one the Haight's biggest draws.

POSITIVELY HAIGHT STREET
1400 Haight St., San Francisco: 415-252-8747
No web site – see sites above in intro.
Tie-dye and Grateful Dead memorabilia along with colorful t-shirts hanging everywhere, reminiscent of the '60s.

PIPE DREAMS
1376 Haight St., San Francisco: 415-431-3553
http://www.pipesinthecity.com
Oldest head shop on Haight Street, looks like it was plucked straight from the '70s.

VERD'S FUNK
1312 Haight St., San Francisco: 415-431-7509
No web site – see sites above in intro.
Trendy fashions, local artists, great designers. A shop with coolness and fun.

HAYES VALLEY SHOPPING
Hayes St. and Gough: San Francisco
www.**hayesvalley**shop.com/
www.**hayesvalley**.com/

The Hayes Valley is a beautiful blend of art and commerce in a small San Francisco neighborhood brimming with art galleries, contemporary boutiques, interior design studios, outdoor cafes and wine bars. This stretch of San Francisco shopping, in view of the San Francisco Symphony and Opera House, is a great place to find out-of-the-ordinary items like, crafted ultra-modern club chairs, black ribboned dancing shoes and a funky tabletop in shocking blue. Hayes Valley does not tolerate chain names or major outfitters that would infringe on the artful and airy style of the neighborhood. Located at 345 Gough Street is Shoppe Unusual, where over 30 local artists' works are on display in one of Hayes Valley's largest and most colorful retail spaces. Some other unique shopping experiences include 560 Hayes Vintage Boutique, Buu, Gimme Shoes and Evelyn's Antique Chinese Furniture. Prices in Hayes Valley are manageable: San Francisco shoppers can splurge on a well-crafted French truffle bag while ordering lunch for two without tipping the financial scales.

BULO
418 Hayes St., San Francisco: 415-255-4939
http://buloshoes.com
Shoes, Bags & Accessories.

OCTAVIA'S HAZE GALLERY
498 Hayes St., San Francisco: 415-255-6818
Art gallery specializing in blown glass and fine art.

VER UNICA
437 B Hayes St., San Francisco: 415-431-0688
http://www.verunicasf.com/verunicasf.com/Home.html
Considered to be one of the tops sources for vintage fashion in the City, Ver Unica also has a mix of new and upcoming designers.

NORTH BEACH SHOPPING
Grant and Columbus Streets: San Francisco
No general web site

North Beach, the unmistakable Italian district of San Francisco, boasts an Italian style and energy that permeates every boutique and restaurant. North Beach is the perfect shopping getaway because visitors will dine as the Romans do while finding unique European-inspired boutiques along Grant Avenue. Old Vogue carries a vintage wardrobe for men and women with the occasional funky piece. InSolent has year-round footwear and for an old Elvis LP then 101 Music is your destination, jammed with more than 10,000 musical items in CD, cassette and LP format. No shopping day is complete without Steps of Rome, where the waiters serve cappuccinos with a flirty wink and call the female patrons "Bellisima."

GRAND IMPORTS
1228 Grant Ave., San Francisco: 415-395-9806
Gifts, jewelry, clothing.

OLD VOGUE
1412 Grant Ave., San Francisco: 415-392-1522
Classic and vintage duds.

TREASURE ISLAND FLEA
Treasure Island off the Bay Bridge: 415-898-0245
www.treasureislandflea.com
On the last weekend of every month (10 to 4) there's a HUGE flea market over on Treasure Island (not really in the North Beach district, but I wasn't sure where else to list this). Lots of food trucks offering a vast array of different kinds of food, from empanadas to burgers to exotic Chinese and Japanese specialties. The artists and designers who exhibit their wares are very often the people who make the stuff, so be sure to show an interest in the work. It will flatter them. By coming out here, you'll also be treated to some of the more stunning views of San Francisco.

MISSION STREET SHOPPING
Valencia and 16th Streets: San Francisco
No general web site

For tourists and San Francisco shoppers with more eclectic and far flung tastes, the Mission is the perfect place to cater to unconventional whims. The Mission a colorful stretch of blocks with offbeat boutiques and funky ethnic clothing and furniture stores. Living up to its catch-all attitude, the Mission offer most anything, but with a funky twist such as mini snakeskin boots for toddlers, white go go boots, velvet hunting hats, and vintage hipster fashion mixed in with discount fabric and bridal stores. However, mixed in with the eccentric is the Mission's predominantly Latino working class which operate authentic bakeries and fresh markets. Standouts include Rayon Vert, the eclectic home and florist shop and Fishbowl, the art and clothing gallery. Eateries add a unique flavor to the Mission with taquerias and fresh produce stands on every corner. What you won't find here are fashionistas wearing the same Gap sweater; the Mission prides itself on its inimitable and colorful style.

FLAX ART & DESIGN
1699 Market St., San Francisco: 415-552-2355
http://flaxart.com
Cards & Stationery, Art Supplies, Framing.

MISSION COMICS & ART
3520 20th St., Suite B, San Francisco: 415-695-1545
http://www.missioncomicsandart.com
Art Galleries, Comic Books.

MULTIKULTI
539 Valencia St., San Francisco: 415-437-1718
No web site
Inexpensive, unique and adorable tights, scarves, sunglasses, costumes, costume jewelry, eyelashes, belly dance gear, playa wear, wigs, hats, and accessories.

MY TRICK PONY
744 Alabama St., San Francisco: 415-861-0595
http://mytrickpony.com
Men's and women's fashions, great for custom t-shirts.

POLK STREET SHOPPING
Polk St. and Broadway: San Francisco
www.**polkst**.com/

Polk Street is one of the most divergent shopping neighborhoods in San Francisco, offering a blend of high-end consignment shops, affordable retail outfits shops and low-end clothing stores. Different tastes and budgets are accommodated on Polk: the outdoor enthusiast will find Lombardi Sports a sports haven, the uber Mom can find pink tees for herself and baby at Girl Stuff, and the socialite looking for an affordable Chanel jacket can stop in at CRIS, an upscale-only consignment store. Polk is best for out-of-town shoppers who like the gritty mixed in with some high style, the upscale with the zany. Just taking a coffee break allows for options: there's a Starbuck's near the legendary Bob's Donut Shop, offering the classic cheap coffee and glazed donut combo. This San Francisco shopping district has one caveat: the best and safest shopping experience on Polk starts just north of California Street.

EDWARD DAVIS LTD.
1829 Polk St., San Francisco: 415-551-1063
No web site
Among the very best art, antiques & collectibles.

FRAME-O-RAMA
1920 Polk St., San Francisco: 415-551-1063
http://www.frame-o-rama.com
Custom and Readymade Picture Framing, Design Services.

SACRAMENTO STREET SHOPPING
Sacramento and Presidio Streets: San Francisco
www.sacramentostreetshop.com/

Sacramento Street shopping is on the cusp between Pacific Heights and Presidio Heights in a quiet residential neighborhood. The main features are the interior decor shops and high-end, but fun, clothing boutiques. Sacramento offers household items from small to large, from cashmere sofa throws and scented Florentine soaps to oversized Persian rugs and 19th century French tables. When done buying for the home, shoppers can indulge their fashion tastes with bathing suits designed by Shoshana at Brown Eyed Girl, a shop designed to look like the interior of a hip apartment, and view Jimmy Choo sandals and Prada heels at Fetish shoes. Sacramento Street is the ultimate deluxe shopping avenue with fantastic finds squeezed into a compact little block.

BATH SENSE
412 Presidio St. (bet. California & Sacramento Sts.), 415-795-3459
http://www.bath-sense.com
Specialties for your bed or your bath.

BETTINA
3615 Sacramento St., San Francisco: 415-563-8002
http://www.bettinasf.com
Fashionable boutique with great selections in all the current trends in clothing and accessories for women.

THE RIBBONERIE
3695 Sacramento St., San Francisco: 415-626-6184
http://www.theribbonerie.com

The largest retailer of specialty ribbons in the West. Large assortment of ribbons and trims.

WOODCHUCK ANTIQUES
3597 Sacramento St., San Francisco: 415-922-6416
http://www.woodchuckantiques.com
Focuses mainly on bronzes, table lamps, and chandeliers, all from the 1870's to the 1930's. Art nouveau and art deco along with neoclassical and the highly collectible Vienna bronzes.

UNION SQUARE SHOPPING
Post St. and Stockton: San Francisco
www.**unionsquareshop**.com/

A lone Corinthian column surrounded by newly installed palm trees marks San Francisco's Mecca for shopaholics. Ringed by Macy's, Saks, Neiman Marcus and Levi's stores along with colorful flower stands and street performers. Surrounding streets feature superstores like Virgin Megastore, Gump's and Britex Fabrics along with boutiques for Coach, Bulgari, Cartier, Thomas Pink, Louis Vuitton, MaxMara, Emporio Armani, Diesel, Prada, Celine, Escada, Gucci, Guess, Hermes, Agnes B., Betsey Johnson and Wilkes Bashford. On the lighter side, DSW is a large discount shoe wharehouse steps from the most expensive shops on Union Square, and Imposter's sells classy faux jewelry.

WESTFIELD SAN FRANCISCO CENTRE
Market St. and Powell: San Francisco
www.**westfield**.com/**sanfrancisco**

For San Francisco visitors and tourists, the opulent Westfield San Francisco Centre mall and its surrounding downtown San Francisco shopping environs (Union Square is just a few blocks away) epitomize the San Francisco shopping experience. A gold and marble stronghold of commercialism, the Westfield San Francisco Centre was guarded by police barricades during the peace protests before the Iraq War, and is home to some of the world's largest American chains, including a five-story Nordstrom's, a two-level Abercrombie & Fitch, numerous outlets found in malls across the country such as Victoria's Secret and Bebe, and including high-end retailers like Kenneth Cole and Club Monaco.

Chapter 7
WINE COUNTRY

Depending on the time of year, there's nothing more fun than taking a trip out to the wine country, especially Napa and Sonoma counties. In fact, after you make your first trip, you'll come back and focus on this special part of America, so completely a world unto itself that there's literally nothing else like it in this country. I am in the wine trade myself (my family produces a fine sparkling wine using grapes from Napa and Sonoma), so I know a little bit about it.

The two counties are quite different in layout and attitude. Though Napa is more famous than Sonoma, winemaking actually began in Sonoma (in 1835) a whole generation before vineyards were planted in the 35-mile lone Napa Valley. And while vineyards line Napa from one end to the other, in Sonoma there still are fields where vineyards have not been planted.

While Napa is narrow and more confined, in Sonoma, the land extends out from the Russian River far and wide, giving you a much more expansive sensation.

Wine lovers didn't really begin flocking to this area until the 1980s, and the lodgings at the time were limited to a few inns and some B&Bs.

These days, however you'll find lodgings to match anywhere in the world, complementing the high quality of the wines produced here.

Nobody thinks of this, but did you know there's a **Veterans Home** in Yountville? Now, I ask you, if you had been in the military, wouldn't you want to retire here?

Lodgings
Restaurants
Cooking Classes
Attractions / Tours
Outlet Stores
Spas

WINE COUNTRY LODGINGS

ARBOR GUEST HOUSE
1436 G St., Napa: 707-252-8144
arborguesthouse.com
The Arbor Guest House Bed & Breakfast has three suites in the main house and two suites in the Carriage House. This timeless estate features an enchanting gazebo and tranquil sitting areas throughout the garden where guests can relax their minds and forget the rush of everyday life, play a mellow game of bocce ball or stroll the beautifully cultivated grounds. Retire to the living room for afternoon wine with nosh or relax and read the paper by the fire.

ANDAZ NAPA
1450 First St., Napa: 707-687-1234
napa.andaz.hyatt.com
Right in downtown Napa, the Andaz makes an excellent choice if you want to explore the 14 tasting rooms in the immediate area featuring some of the best wines in California. All the usual amenities. (A Hyatt property.)

AUBERGE DU SOLEIL RESORT
180 Rutherford Hill Rd., Rutherford: 707-963-1211
aubergedusoleil.com
Since 1985, this has been a top place to stay. They have a collection of sun- and earth-toned rooms and suites, each featuring French doors opening onto private terraces, cozy fireplaces and sensuous elements such as private soaking tubs for two. For the Auberge's signature style of soft-spoken luxury, the partners tapped renowned designer Michael Taylor, who infused his dramatic California style with the essence of Provence. Full spa services. (Try the milk chocolate bath in-suite, for a touch of decadence.) Certainly one of Napa's most luxurious resorts, with one of the area's best restaurants, the **Bistro & Bar**. Since it's really pricey, check out the Bistro first. Here you can order a couple of small plates to taste (from $6) and get a glass of wine (from $9), and not break the budget while taking advantage of the sunset on the terrace or the fire crackling inside.

AUBERGE ON THE VINEYARD
29955 River Rd., Cloverdale: 707-894-5956
www.sonomabedbreakfastinnwinecountry.com
Though the original Victorian building that stood here went up in 1885, it burned down and the current house constructed in 1910, so you still have as very Victorian feel to your surroundings. You can stay in one of the rooms in the old house, or choose the "Carriage House" where they have

several other nicely appointed rooms. Very nice breakfasts. This is one of the oldest B&Bs in the area. Lots of activities, including workshops where they will show you how to prune the vines, blend wines and enjoy barrel tastings. Very hands-on and lots of fun.

BARDESSONO
6526 Yount St., Yountville: 707-204-6000
www.bardessono.com/spa/
They have 62 rooms here in downtown Yountville. Each is designed for in-room spa services. The menu in the restaurant here is based on local, farm-fresh ingredients. A real treat is the rooftop pool where you can also dine. I've been all over the world, but I've never seen a menu item reading "freshly dug carrot salad." I'm tempted to write that it's "so freshly dug you can still taste the dirt on the carrot," but I'm not. (In any case, go for the parsnip soup—it's really good.) They have a wide selection of fish here, and it's painstakingly prepared, but don't overlook the lamb T-bone: you almost never see that cut (it's served with fennel, squash and "saffron spaetzle," and it's excellent).

BEAZLEY HOUSE
1910 1st St., Napa: 707-257-1649
beazleyhouse.com
"Napa's first & still its finest bed & breakfast inn."
The Beazley House is just a short walk from the newly revitalized downtown Napa riverfront, the Napa Valley Opera House, the Napa Valley Wine Train, fine dining, shopping, and Napa's Oxbow Market. The downtown Napa location is a perfect "home base" from which to explore wineries, vineyards, more restaurants, and the picturesque Napa Valley.

Construction within the historic mansion was challenging. The Beazleys strove to maintain the original feel while accommodating the needs of today's Napa travelers. Private baths were cleverly fitted into the existing bedrooms and all per Napa County building codes and regulations.

Beazley House is dog friendly, provides free wireless Internet access, has delicious breakfasts made in-house, and features exquisite gardens, comfortable rooms, and gracious hosts, Jim and Carol Beazley.

CALISTOGA RANCH
580 Lommel Rd., Calistoga: 800-942-4220
www.calistogaranch.com/

The "lodges" here offer private patios, fireplaces, great views of the 150+ acre compound. Oak groves abound, so you're really quite in the country. Very posh. Yoga deck. Expensive, of course, starting from $900. Very private, facilities and grounds top-notch. (Take a look into their wine cave. Kind of eerie.)

CANDLELIGHT INN
1045 Easum Dr., Napa: 707-257-3717
candlelightinn.com
Candlelight Inn — a luxurious Napa Valley bed and breakfast. Located near downtown Napa, this lovely 1929 English Tudor inn is centrally located to all the wonders of wine country, yet oh, so far away.
Secluded beneath towering redwood trees along the banks of the Napa Creek, Candlelight Inn rests on an acre of quiet, park-like grounds. A romantic and restful backyard delights sun seekers with manicured gardens and a gorgeous swimming pool.

CARNEROS INN
4048 Sonoma Hwy., Napa: 707-299-4900
www.thecarnerosinn.com
You can see for miles from the vantage point of the rise where the inn is situated. There are almost no trees obstructing the view, which gives the place a rather Spartan feel, but it's quite luxurious. Great lodgings, restaurant and bar. Open and airy, lots of windows.

CEDAR GABLES INN
486 Coombs St., Napa: 707-224-7969
cedargablesinn.com
Cedar Gables Inn, a luxurious 10,000 square foot Napa Valley Bed and Breakfast mansion, where enchantment, romance and history await you in Downtown Napa. Treat yourself to an unforgettable B&B experience as you indulge in delicious three course gourmet breakfasts, evening hors d'oeuvres, wine tasting and the ultimate in hospitality. Be whisked away to Renaissance England at one of the grandest and most treasured bed and breakfast inns in Northern California!

Napa Cooking Classes
Paired with outstanding wines from the best wine producing region in the world, the Cedar Gables Inn Cooking School offers the ultimate Napa Culinary Experience: Hands on cooking classes with top notch chefs from the area. Following the class you will enjoy the fruits of your labor by feasting on your creations and delicious wines in the Inn's elegant dining room.

CHELSEA GARDEN INN
1443 Second St., Calistoga: 707-942-0948
chelseagardeninn.com
Set among lush garden paths, Chelsea Garden Inn is a wonderfully unique Napa Valley inn featuring one-bedroom suites with private entrances, private baths, and fireplaces. With a secluded seasonal pool and jasmine-lined walkways, you'll renew yourself in an environment created to revive and enliven the soul. Whimsical touches and bold shades of color blend with fine linens, down pillows, and other amenities in every private suite.

GOLDEN HAVEN HOT SPRINGS SPA AND RESORT
1713 Lake St., Calistoga: 707-942-8000
goldenhaven.com
Calistoga Golden Haven Hot Springs Spa is nestled in the heart of California's Napa Valley wine country and makes the perfect Calistoga spa getaway. Come and experience the magic of the Calistoga hot springs water and rejuvenating spa treatments. After a day of touring Napa Valley, you can swim in their hot springs pool, relax on the sun deck under the California sun, and rejuvenate with their famous Calistoga spa treatments.

HENNESSEY HOUSE
1727 Main St., Napa: 707-226-3774
hennesseyhouse.com
Stroll to historic downtown Napa's outstanding restaurants, lovely galleries and shops, theaters, the Wine Train, and the Opera House.
Napa's world-class wineries are just minutes away from our Napa Valley bed and breakfast by car.
Hennessey House, located on a residential portion of Main Street, is the perfect home base for exploring all that Napa Valley has to offer.

HOTEL YOUNTVILLE
6462 Washington St., Yountville: 707-967-7900
www.hotelyountville.com/
You don't even need a car hen you get here. So many great places to eat are within walking distance, you could spend a week here and never get in a car. Lots of little boutiques for shopping, and 4 wine tasting rooms nearby. Their concierges will help you navigate the Napa area if you want them to. Free bikes. Let them know what you're interested in before you arrive and they'll map out what you need to do to see it all. **Spa AcQua** is located here. They have 6 treatment rooms, 2 couple's "spa suites" featuring Vichy showers, luxurious double hydrotherapy tubs and

fireplaces. Decadent? Oh, yes. Check out their web site to see the kind of specially priced packages they offer that might apply to you when you travel.

INDIAN SPRINGS
1712 Lincoln Ave., Calistoga: 707-942-4913
indianspringscalistoga.com
As you turn in to Indian Springs' palm tree-lined drive, you're entering a truly historic spa resort. Situated in Calistoga at the northern end of the Napa Valley, Indian Springs Resort and Spa is California's oldest continuously operating pool and spa facility. Situated on 16 beautiful acres planted with olive and palm trees, roses and lavender, the property is blessed with four thermal geysers that produce an extraordinary supply of rich mineral water. Another prized asset is the vast, natural deposit of pure volcanic ash on the acreage. These unique elements have long inspired a tradition of healing and renewal on this very site.

THE INK HOUSE
1575 St. Helena Hwy. S., St. Helena: 707-963-3890
www.inkhouseinn.com/
Treat yourself to Victorian elegance in the midst of the Napa Valley's world famous wine growing region. Among the vineyards and neighbors to some of the finest wineries and restaurants, a stay at the Ink House is a nostalgic return to an era long past with all the conveniences of modern comfort. Built in 1884, by Theron H. Ink, this grand and historic landmark home is listed on the National Register of Historic Places. Here at his "Helios Ranch", Ink, a true pioneer, lived with his wife and children and presided over many Napa Valley ventures. This Italianate Victorian style home offers two first floor parlors, with antiques, fireplace, circa 1870 pump organ, crystal chandeliers and original stained glass.

INN ON RANDOLPH
411 Randolph St., Napa: 707-257-2886
innonrandolph.com
If you're looking for a Napa Valley Bed and Breakfast to enjoy a romantic getaway or relaxing home base for wine tasting, fine dining or recreation, look no further than the Inn on Randolph. For over 16 years guests of the inn have enjoyed our location, amenities, privacy and service, all of which set the stage for an unforgettable Wine Country vacation. Ideally located in the historic district of downtown Napa, it's only a short walk to more than 16 tasting rooms, popular restaurants, evening activities and local events.

KENWOOD INN
10400 Sonoma Hwy., Kenwood: 707.833.1293
www.kenwoodinn.com
This charming place in Sonoma is nestled in the Valley of the Moon surrounded by vineyards, oak groves, walnut orchards and fruit trees. Nothing here is left to chance. The smallest detail is seen to. Here you'll find a restful hideaway with only 29 rooms and suites, each, the Kenwood Inn and Spa is designed with hand-crafted artistry and a sophisticated sensibility, each with fireplaces, featherbeds, Italian linens for bed and bath, free breakfast, robes for lounging and twice daily housekeeping service.

The Spa at Kenwood has vinotherapy body treatments, "iS" clinical facial treatments, Intraceuticals oxygen treatments, Éminence body treatments, therapeutic massage.

The restaurant here serves breakfast, lunch and dinner in a cozy atmosphere. Creative salads like persimmon with roasted quince, mache and pomegranate vinaigrette; or San Daniele prosciutto with arugula, parmesan, pears and pine nuts. But there's heartier fare: lamb chops and a prime ribeye with romesco butter, bacon lardon potatoes, telaggio creamed baby spinach that'll melt in your mouth.

Mobil 4 star rated spa since 2004. This place has garnered top ratings: "Top 55 Spas in North America, in the Caribbean, and at Sea" from Condé Nast Traveler Reader's Poll. (They scored a perfect 100 for setting and service.) Also, the 2007 SpaFinder's Reader's Poll: awarded "Best Accommodations" and "Best Interior Design"

Spa Magazine 2010 Silver Sage Award; Favorite Spas for Couples-US; Favorite Resort & Hotel Spas-Northern California & Pacific Northwest.

LAVENDER
2020 Webber Ave., Yountville: 800-522-4140
lavendernapa.com
What they've achieved here is a combination of modern luxuries and top-notch services and given it all the look and feel of a B&B. "Conde Nast Traveler" voted it one the "Top 50 Small Hotels," and that's no accident. An old house forms the center of complex of 4 buildings. There's a wraparound porch, an enclosed verandah where breakfast is served. They've made every effort to give you the feeling you're in Provence. (And they come damn close.)

MEADOWOOD
900 Meadowood Lane, St. Helena: 800-458-8080
www.meadowood.com

Luxurious resort in a splendid country setting. They do everything here: weddings, sporting events (they have a pool, tennis courts, golf), conferences, events and a wide variety of seasonal offerings (like a Thanksgiving special that's very nice). It's one thing to see how "the other half" live, but here you can see how they relax.

From $650 to over $1,000 per night. (If you're a foodie, you'll want to know that **The Restaurant at Meadowood** got 3 stars from Michelin.)

THE NAPA INN
1137 Warren St., Napa: 707.257.1444
napainn.com

The Napa Inn is a place of serenity where your cares and worries will melt away as you bask in the warmth and ambiance of this lovely Napa Bed and Breakfast Wine Country Inn. All of our 14 Napa Wine Country guest rooms and suites are individually decorated. Each has its own private bathroom and fireplace. All Napa Inn guest rooms have AC, cable TV w/VCR, wireless internet service and many have two-person whirlpool tubs and all have showers. The Napa Inn observes Eco-friendly practices.

A gourmet candlelight breakfast is served each morning in the Napa Inn dining room or on the garden patio. Enjoy evening wine and refreshments at this romantic Napa Valley Wine Country Inn. Coffee, teas and waters always available at Napa Inn.

OLD WORLD INN
1301 Jefferson St., Napa: 707-257-0112
oldworldinn.com

As one of Napa's first bed and breakfasts, the Old World Inn is known for two things: homestyle food and friendliness. Guests are treated to a gourmet's repast, from freshly baked chocolate chip cookies upon check-in, to a 5:30 wine reception, to mouthwatering chocolate desserts when they return back to the Inn each evening. Each morning begins with the smell of freshly ground coffee (or teas) and a two-course gourmet breakfast that gets you ready for a day of wine tasting.

PETIT LOGIS
6527 Yount St., Yountville: 877-944-2332
www.petitlogis.com/

Completely seductive inn with only 5 rooms. It's not a B&B in the sense that there's no breakfast. (But there's the famous **Bouchon Bakery** just next door where you can get a REALLY great morning snack! They open at 7 a.m., by the way.) The rooms here, while comfy and rustic (they even have fireplaces), still offer completely updated amenities: big bathrooms, jacuzzi tubs, refrigerators, wireless Internet. Great restaurants like the **French Laundry** are just down the street.

VILLAGIO
6481 Washington St., Yountville-Napa Valley: 707-944-8877
villagio.com
Located on the 23-acre Vintage Estate, Villagio Inn & Spa has been dubbed by Town & Country Magazine as a "pleasure seeker's heaven." This Tuscan-inspired Yountville hotel property features flowing water fountain pathways weaved throughout lush Mediterranean-style gardens. Experience the warmth and richness of Villagio's guestrooms and suites that the San Francisco Chronicle Magazine describes as "massive, terribly tasteful and terribly elegant."

RESTAURANTS / WINE BARS

WINE GUIDE
It never hurts to keep current on the latest vintages, so I always recommend you get the new edition of Hugh Johnson's Pocket Wine Book 2013. It runs to some 300 pages. (You can get the ebook at online retailers for about $10, or a used hardcover copy for about $7 + shipping, depending on your preference. Hugh Johnson is a towering figure among wine writers. I like him a little better than Robert Parker.

ANGELE
540 Main St., Napa: 707-252-8115
angelerestaurant.com
CUISINE: French
DRINKS: Full Bar
SERVING: Lunch / Dinner
Has a menu that layers elements from traditional recipes with contemporary influences. Its focus on rich and soothing French cuisine ranges from the classic simplicity of fresh, seasonal salads to the robust balance of bœuf bourguignon.
Whether seated at a table in the dining room, at the full bar or outside on the terrace overlooking the Napa River, enjoy lunch and dinner surrounded by a simple, familial setting.

BACK ROOM WINES
1000 Main St., Suite 100, Napa: 707-226-1378
backroomwines.com/

Great series of wine tastings and other wine-related events. Perfect store to buy wine to take back home.

BISTRO DON GIOVANNI
4110 Howard Ln., Napa: 707-224-3300
bistrodongiovanni.com
CUISINE: Italian
DRINKS: Full Bar
SERVING: Lunch/ Dinner
The best tasting meals are prepared simply, and with the freshest ingredients. They source their herbs, vegetables and produce from local farmers and support ranches that raise humanely-treated, free-roaming livestock and poultry. All of the menu items are inspired by the bounty of the region and prepared with utmost attention to detail. Donna's way of selecting and combining seasonal products to highlight pure, robust flavors in an ever changing variety has drawn a steady stream of loyal diners. Great wine list, of course.

BISTRO SABOR
1126 First St., Napa: 707-252-0555
http://bistrosabor.com
Here you'll get the kind of street food you only find in Latin America. Really delivious ceviches (Peruvian style), *posole* (a Mexican stew) and *pupusas* (thin tortilla filled snacks from El Savador). every Saturday night from 10 to 1, things get busy with Salsa, Merengue, Cumbia, Bachata and Reggaeton. You're invited to DANCE! No cover charge.

CELADON
500 Main St., Napa: 707-254-9690
celadonnapa.com
CUISINE: American/ Seafood
DRINKS: Full Bar
SERVING: Lunch/ Dinner
Enjoy Celadon's award-winning 'Global Comfort Food' in their beautiful dining room or on the lovely courtyard. The seasonally influenced menu features flavors from the Mediterranean, Asia, and the Americas.

LA TOQUE
1314 McKinstry St., Napa: 707-257-5157
latoque.com
CUISINE: American/ French
DRINKS: Full Bar

SERVING: Dinner
The menu evolves constantly to show off each season's finest ingredients. They have developed a network of local farmers and purveyors who supply them with some of the finest foods in the world. The Options menu is presented in three sections from which you can create your own multi-course experience. Their Chef's Tasting Menu and Vegetable Tasting Menu are presented in a fixed format of five courses.

NEELA'S
975 Clinton St., Napa: 707-226-9988
neelasnapa.com
CUISINE: Indian
DRINKS: Beer/ Wine
SERVING: Lunch/ Dinner
Neela's menu features the many different provinces of India—vegetarian dishes from the south and tandoor-cooked dishes from the north, as well as chaat (street foods) and classic dishes of the British Raj—all made with the freshest ingredients available to create bright, home-style fare. Neela's also features Bollywood music videos in the bar, plus a weekly Wednesday vegetarian tasting menu and Thursday Bread Night—a selection of stuffed flat breads served with salads and raita.

OENOTRI
425 First St., Napa: 707-252-1022
oenotri.com
CUISINE: Italian
DRINKS: Full Bar
SERVING: Lunch/ Dinner
Oenotri is an Italian restaurant in downtown Napa featuring a daily changing menu driven by ingredients that are local, fresh and in season. They celebrate culinary traditions rarely seen elsewhere in California — the specialties of Sicily, Campania, Calabria, Basilicata and Puglia. Salumi is handcrafted in house, and their pasta is made fresh daily. As part of their goal to serve quality artisanal pizza, they imported a wood-fueled Acino oven from Naples to bake authentic pizza Napoletana.

PEARL
1339 Pearl St., Napa: 707-224-9161
therestaurantpearl.com
CUISINE: American
DRINKS: Beer/ Wine
SERVING: Lunch/ Dinner

Pearl is a casual bistro just off the main streets of downtown Napa. Proprietors Nickie and Peter Zeller have created an energetic and exciting space with soaring ceilings, vibrant local artwork and comfortable seating both indoors and on the front patio. As its namesake suggests, Pearl starts by offering oysters, raw on the half shell, roasted with salsa verde and feta. Other starters include soft tacos with ginger marinated flank steak and house made tortillas, crab cakes and Guerrero style corn on the cob with chili cream, cojita cheese and lime. A variety of sandwiches served on house focaccia, soft polenta with sautéed seasonal vegetables and roasted tomato sauce, daily fish specials, Jose's chicken verde, and the famous triple double frenched pork chop with apple brine are a sampling of entree choices. Finish your meal with a seasonal fruit crisp, johnnycake cobbler, pineapple upside down cake, or a variety of house made sorbets and ice creams.

THE RESTAURANT AT MEADOWOOD
900 Meadowood Lane, St. Helena: 800-458-8080
www.meadowood.com
Black truffle gnocchi with parsnip Mousse and brown butter, king salmon with beets, Pacific black cod with white asparagus, chanterelles, bonito. There's also a smoke chicken that unusual. (This place got 3 stars from Michelin.)

VINTNER'S COLLECTIVE TASTING ROOM
1245 Main St., Napa: 707-255-7150
www.**vintnerscollective**.com
Another great spot for tasting the wines of many different wineries, all under the roof of an historic building that has been restored. The building has an interesting history all its own: it formerly housed a brothel, a brewery, a laundry, a meat company and a saloon.

ZUZU
829 Main St., Napa: 707-224-8555
zuzunapa.com
CUISINE: Spanish Tapas
DRINKS: Beer/ Wine
SERVING: Lunch/ Dinner/ Weekends dinner only
The restaurant offers a modern, California version of tapas along with some traditional offerings based on the cuisines of Spain, Portugal and the Mediterranean. The Chefs of ZuZu are inspired by fresh, seasonal ingredients and places an emphasis on using organic and sustainable produce, seafood and meats.

CALISTOGA RESTAURANTS

ALL SEASONS BISTRO
1400 Lincoln Ave., Calistoga: 707-942-9111
allseasonsnapavalley.net
CUISINE: American
DRINKS: Beer/ Wine
SERVING: Lunch/ Dinner
Passionate about fine wines and steeped in a history of family restaurateurs, Alex and Gayle were among the first wave of food and wine professionals in Napa Valley's "modern" era, opening their first restaurant here in 1976. Theirs was among the first restaurants in the United States to receive the Wine Spectator's prestigious "Grand Award." The restaurant has been praised in the San Francisco Chronicle, the Zagat Guide and the very recent Michelin Guide to the San Francisco Bay Area. They're proud to display their "People Love Us On Yelp" decal, where readers gave All Seasons 4.5 of 5 stars. They continue to incorporate their personal beliefs into the business, emphasizing seasonal and regional ingredients, sustainable farming and fishing, all coupled with the best small production, hand crafted wines.

BAROLO
1457 Lincoln Ave., Calistoga: 707-942-9900
barolocalistoga.com
CUISINE: American/ Italian
DRINKS: Full Bar
SERVING: Dinner
Witty sophistication meets rustic hip with Barolo's unique mix of simple food done simply well coupled with an unpretentious and approachable local wine list. Great music and a cool, laid-back vibe are a hallmark of this popular Calistoga eatery known for its great food and friendly service.

BOSKO'S TRATTORIA
1364 Lincoln Ave., Calistoga: 707-942-9088
boskos.com
CUISINE: Italian/ Pizza
DRINKS: Beer/ Wine
SERVING: Lunch/ Dinner

Italian comfort food in the upper Napa Valley. With its spectacular setting, simple Italian classics, exciting value wine priced menu, warm and friendly service and large servings at reasonable prices. Bosko's sets the standard for casual Italian dining.

FLATIRON GRILL
1440 Lincoln Ave., Calistoga: 707-942-1220
flatirongrill.com
CUISINE: Steakhouse
DRINKS: Full Bar
SERVING: Dinner
Opened in 2001. Having restored the interior, recreated the private dining space and completely changing the atmosphere, the FlatIron Grill has developed a dining destination for Calistogans and day-trippers alike.

SOLBAR
In **Solage Resortggff**
755 Silverado Tr., Calistoga: 866-942-7442
solagecalistoga.com
CUISINE: American
DRINKS: Full Bar
SERVING: Breakfast/ Lunch/Dinner
"Hands down, the Maitake mushroom pizza at Solbar is the Napa Valley's best up-valley option for great pizza, and it's the only pizza available on the Silverado Trail, as far as I know. The dough at Solbar is based upon a biga-style starter, which cultivates and propagates the yeasts, developing a more complex flavor within the crust. Traditionally, Italian bakers use a biga starter for making ciabatta bread, and Solbar's pizza crust definitely features some ciabatta-like characteristics within the crumb.

YOUNTVILLE

BOUCHON BAKERY
6528 Washington St., Yountville: 707-944-2253
bouchonbakery.com/
CUISINE: French bakery
DRINKS: no booze
SERVING: 7 a.m. to 7 p.m.
All foodies know that this bakery is owned by the famed **Thomas Keller**, owner of the **French Laundry**. Come here for baked goods prepared using the classic recipes: pastries, Viennoiserie, cookies, macaroons. But also for breakfast, confections, quiche, sandwiches, salads, picnic baskets, even

treats for your pets.

FRENCH LAUNDRY
6640 Washington St. (at Creek St.), Yountville: 707-944-2380
www.frenchlaundry.com
CUISINE: American; French
DRINKS: beer & wine
SERVING: lunch Friday-Sunday 11-1; dinner nightly from 5:30; DRESS CODE: don't even think about jeans or shorts or slovenly dress; men ought to bring a jacket, even a tie if you want to fit in.
Get ready for the meal of your life. All professional foodies know about this very expensive Thomas Keller eatery located in a wonderful setting in the wine country. Reserve as far ahead as you can, because it's murder to get in. But once you do, you'll be treated to one of the best dining experiences of your life. You do tend to get the feeling you're in church when you're here, so reverent are the diners and so focused are the staff. But just surrender to Keller's prix-fixe menu of 9 courses. You'll be amused at the tiny portions (you don't exactly need a microscope to see them), but they all add up to a very filling meal by the time you finish. And, much more important, an experience you'll *never* forget. When Keller dies, people will weep. $270.

COOKING CLASSES

CASA LANA B&B
1316 S. Oak St., Calistoga: 877-968-2665
www.casalana.com
Casa Lana offers "Gourmet Retreats" for home cooks and food enthusiasts. The hands-on classes are taught in the B&B's professionally equipped kitchen and range in length from a 5-hour class to a full 5-day Culinary Learning Vacation. The small class size (up to 8 people) provides personalized attention for each participant. Private classes and Team Building sessions are also available.

THE CULINARY INSTITUTE OF AMERICA AT GREYSTONE
2555 Main St., Helena: 707-967-1010
ciachef.edu/restaurants/wsgr
One- and Two-Day Programs. Invigorating Mornings in the Kitchen. You'll don chef's whites and head right into the kitchen for lecture, hands-on cooking, and food and wine pairings. There's no shortage of fascinating topics to explore, from the cuisines of Northern California to healthy sustainable eating and live-fire grilling.

You'll enjoy lecture, hands-on cooking, and a wine tasting and sensory analysis session, and come away with a better understanding of the flavors of California.

Tuition one-day: $495 per person. Tuition two-days (includes off-campus visits and dinners): $1,995.00

ATTRACTIONS / TOURS

BEAU WINE TOURS
1680 Pear Tree Ln., Napa: 707-257-0887
beauwinetours.com

Looking for something a little more economical than your own private limo? Interested in meeting other people and making friends on a fun Daily Tour? Beau Wine Tours now offers the ultimate daily wine tour in the Napa Valley! Enjoy a full day of wine tasting and making new friends as you tour one of the world's most famous wine regions in a Luxury Limousine or Limo Bus! During this fun and informative tour, you will learn about the local history and geography that makes Napa Valley such a popular destination for wine lovers and foodies all over the world. Each tour starts with complimentary champagne served on-board one of their luxurious vehicles, as you meet fellow wine enthusiasts and wine curious guests. Your friendly and knowledgeable tour guide will take you to four exceptional boutique wineries known for great tasting wine and warm hospitality. You will have many opportunities to take pictures of the majestic scenery, unique artwork, beautiful landscaping, and architecture. Your guide will also be happy to take photos of you and the group at each winery throughout the day. Each tour includes a catered picnic lunch from the famous Girl & the Fig Restaurant, served at one of the many hidden-gem locations in the valley (usually among vineyard views, garden terraces or wine cellars depending on weather). Our delicious and hearty lunches are served "family style" allowing everyone to pick and choose from a variety of sandwiches, side salads, and desserts. $99.00 Per Person. (Does not include tasting fees.)

CALISTOGA FARMER'S MARKET
1235 Washington St., Calistoga: 707-942-8892
calistogafarmersmarket.org

Saturdays, 8:30 a.m. - 12 Noon; May 7 through October 29. Sharpsteen Plaza located across from the City Hall in downtown Calistoga.

CASTELLO DI AMOROSA
4045 St. Helena Hwy., Calistoga: 707-967-6272
www.**castellodiamorosa**.com

A crazy winemaker, Dario Sattui, for all his life in love with medieval architecture, built this fantastic castle of over 100 rooms (I think I remember that it has over 120,000 square feet), all in the style of the ancient castle-fortresses of Northern Italy. An $18 admission fee gives you not only a tour of the place, but also a tasting of 5 of their wines. There's a Knight's Room featuring frescoes, a torture chamber, a chapel (actually used for weddings and whatnot), extensive wine cellars—all of it will give you a feeling that you're FAR away from the Napa Valley.

GOURMET NAPA WALKING TOUR
415-312-1119
COST: $68 per person
gourmetwalks.com
There is more to Napa than just wine tasting! Welcome to the FIRST culinary walking tour in Wine Country, for those who know that California cuisine is just as sought after as its wine. This tour will delight your taste buds as you explore revitalized downtown Napa with fellow foodies. They will share the fascinating history of this beautiful riverfront town, one where celebrity chefs intermingle with organic farmers and boutique winemakers. They will begin at the new Oxbow Market, where a seasonal bounty of California specialty foods and produce awaits you. Your tour will cross the Napa River and visit 19th century historic buildings that weathered Prohibition to showcase the latest trends in California food and wine. You'll leave the tour with a carefully curated list of Wine Country restaurant recommendations and recipes for your next meal. NOTE: Customers must be over 21 and bring valid id to participate in wine tastings.

HALL RUTHERFORD
56 Auberge Rd., Rutherford: 707-967-0700
COST: $40 per person
hallwines.com/hall-rutherford
Hall Rutherford is Craig and Kathryn Hall's stunning winery amid the legendary Sacrashe vineyard. State-of-the-art vision, timeless artisanship and gracious hospitality are showcased in every luxurious detail. Completed in March of 2005, this high-tech facility has been carefully designed for the production of small-lot red wine. Custom made three-to-six-ton fermenters afford their winemakers great flexibility and precision handling of vineyard blocks and the ability to micro-manage every aspect of the winemaking process. Unlike the Halls' St. Helena property, which is able to handle more significant quantities of grapes during harvest, this compact gravity-flow winery is dedicated solely to the production of rare and single vineyard red wines. The winery's 14,000 square feet of caves

were designed and built by hand by Friedrich Gruber of Gutenstein Austria. The caves are finished with handmade Austrian brick recovered from sites in and around Vienna and showcases select works from the Halls' art collection. Deep inside the caves resides a dazzling reception area for private tastings and entertaining. The room's spectacular chandelier, designed by Donald Lipski and Jonquil LeMaster, is dressed in hundreds of Swarovski crystals. Tours of the winery offer guests a truly world-class winery experience to include a tasting of HALL's most regaled wines along with an intimate tour through the property and caves.

NAPA RIVER ADVENTURES' GUIDED RIVER BOAT CRUISES
816 Third St., Napa: 707-224 9080
COST: $55 per person, $25 children under 12. Gratuities are welcomed.
napariveradventures.com
Their captains give an incredibly in-depth, insider tour of the Napa River and everything that is connected to it. All cruises are aboard the ElectraCraft electric boat, which comfortably seats up to 11 passengers. Seating is limousine-style and the wrap-around windows provide panoramic views from every seat. Guests are encouraged to bring beverages and snacks to enjoy during their cruise. Your Napa River Adventures cruise begins with a narrative of the Napa River and the impact it has had on the local community. As they head North along the Napa River passing through the recently restored wetlands and head towards historic downtown Napa, you will be able to see remnants of the past and understand how present changes will affect the future of Napa. The many species of birds provide topics of interest and are beautiful elements in the sweeping vistas of the valley. You will note the change in the temperature, wind along the cruise - and understand the unique micro-climates that enable Napa Valley to produce exceptional wines. Tides and times permitting, they will also pass Copia: The American Center for Wine, Food and Art, and the Napa Yacht Club.

NAPA DOWNTOWN FARMERS' MARKET
500 First St., Napa: 707-501-3087
www.napafarmersmarket.com
The Napa Certified Farmers Market has been bringing fresh, local produce, specialty foods and artisan crafts to the City of Napa, California, for more than 20 years. Tuesdays and Saturdays from 7:30 a.m. until noon

NAPA VALLEY BALLOONS
6795 Washington St., Yountville: 707-944-0228
COST: $240 per person, add $10 for in-flight photo

napavalleyballoons.com
Voted Best Balloon Ride" 1996-2010. Featured on the Today Show, Oprah and the Travel Channel. The company trusted to fly Chelsea Clinton! Pre-flight & Post-flight Breakfast and Champagne Celebration. Comfortable State-of-the-Art Aircraft.

The award winning Napa Valley Balloons, Inc. has been flying hot air balloons over the Napa Valley for over 28 years. We have FAA certified pilots and aircraft, a professional staff and an impeccable safety record with thousands of satisfied adventurers experiencing the pleasure of hot air ballooning with Napa Valley Balloons, Inc.

NAPA VALLEY BIKE TOURS
6795 Washington Street, Bldg. B, Yountville: 707-944-295
COST: Fees vary depending on package. Rates start at $89 per person.
napavalleybiketours.com
Napa Valley Bike Tours is a full-service bike tour company located in the heart of the Napa Valley. They have been guiding bike tours visiting Napa Valley wineries since 1987. They offer single-day guided winery tours by bike, self-guided winery tours by bike and bike rentals, as well as custom Napa Valley vacation packages.

NAPA VALLEY OPERA HOUSE
1030 Main St., Napa: 707.226.7372
nvoh.org
Napa Valley Opera house is the jewel of the valley that showcases excellence in music and performing arts for audiences of all ages including world-class musical theatre, plays, chamber music, jazz, opera, dance and family programs.

NAPA VALLEY WINE TRAIN
1275 McKinstry St., Napa: 800-427-4124
COST: Varies upon lunch/ dinner and car chosen to ride in
winetrain.com
The tracks upon which the Napa Valley Wine Train runs were originally built in the 1860s to bring guests to the hot spring resort town of Calistoga. While the track to Calistoga no longer exists, much of the rest of the route of the Napa Valley Wine Train is unchanged. Due to the immense influence that rail transport had over the development of the communities and wineries of the Napa Valley, there is no shortage of sights to see during the 3-hour journey to St. Helena. Five towns; Napa, Yountville, Oakville,

Rutherford, and St. Helena; and numerous wineries can be seen through the large picture windows on board the Wine Train. **VISTA DOME -** Intimate, special and above the crowd. Almost 180-degree Napa Valley vistas under the antique dome windows. Enjoy wine pairing events and romantic moonlight dinners. $129 per person. **GOURMET EXPRESS -** Relive the luxury and tradition of railroad dining as the steward seats you in the Gourmet car. White linen service for half your journey. The other? The comfort of the lounge car. $99 per person. **SILVERADO -** Taste the barbeque side of Napa Valley gourmet in the Silverado car. This open air railcar exudes a relaxed atmosphere, with a western theme and sliding windows. $89 per person.

Take the Ferry from San Francisco. Getting here from San Francisco could not be easier - or more pleasant. Hop on a ferry and enjoy a Bay cruise on your way to the Wine Train.

Must make reservations at least a day in advance.

The San Francisco- Napa Connection is $45 per person, available only with their lunch trains. Reservations Required. Leave San Francisco at 8:30, be back by 7:00. Depending on the time of year, you might take the Ferry or the Bus. Check the "Mode of Transportation Table" for details. Both the Ferry and the Bus will drop you off in Vallejo where you will board the Napa Valley Wine Train Shuttle.

RAYMOND VINEYARDS
849 Zinfandel Lane, St. Helena: 707-963-3141
www.raymondvineyards.com
While other wineries have their "tasting rooms," the folks here at Raymond have gone all out to create a dizzying array of feel-good places for you to experience their wines. They have the Crystal Room, the Barrel Room, the Library, the Theatre of Nature, the Rutherford Room and the Corridor of Senses. In the Crystal Room, for example, they have a collection of old decanters you have to see. A crystal chandelier (by Baccarat) hangs above you. You're flanked by stainless steel walls and a mirrored bar. In the Red Room club (membership is $500 for a year, and you can bring up to 3 guests), you can slip into a private lounge where you can play billiards, drink wine, use a vintage pinball machine and enjoy the plushness of more red velvet than you ever thought you'd see.

WINE COUNTRY BUS TOURS
415-353-5310

COST: $75 Adult, $73 Senior, $45 Child 5-11
www.supersightseeing.com
Napa and Sonoma are world famous for their fine wine and beautiful scenery. Learn about wine from our expert guides as you travel north to California's Premiere wine country. You'll learn the areas' history of wine making, from the early Spanish missionaries who brought grape vines from Europe to the Forty-Niners who served wines in their saloons. You will tour wineries and see how grapes are picked, crushed, blended and bottled. You'll walk through beautiful vineyards with your tour guide and then taste the finished product – wine tasting fees included. There will be time for lunch at Historical Sonoma Square or Vintage 1870 in the heart of Napa. ALL TOURS include pick-up and drop-off at most San Francisco Hotels. Approx. 9 hours. Departs: 9 AM.

SAFARI WEST
3115 Porter Creek Rd., Santa Rosa: 707-579-2551
COST: Varies upon season. Starting at Adults $68; Children 3-12 $30; Infants 1-2 $10. safariwest.com
Here in the heart of California's wine country... in the field of wheat-colored grass, on the slopes of rolling green hills, among the trees and ranches and vineyards is where you will find the essence and spirit of Africa. Not a zoo...not a drive through park...this is the home of Nancy and Peter Lang. Come through the gate and be transported into an exotic, new world. A captivating tapestry of raw sounds and earthy smells; a magic place with the sights and sounds of the Serengeti where the air is filled with melodious chirps from the aviary, squawking calls from gregarious parrots, and a occasional lemur screech. An African style oasis where guests experience a rare sense of freedom and gain renewed inspiration. Enjoy all the creature comforts when you spend the night in one of their luxury tents— "It's like having a tent over your room!" Pale-green canvas walls enclose plush beds, hot showers and rustic but elegant trappings. There are polished wood floors, custom wood-slab countertops in the private bathrooms and one-of-a kind hand hewn furniture. There is nothing more magical than falling asleep to the sounds of a kookaburra and waking to the resounding love-songs of the sarus cranes. Removed from televisions, computer screens and even cell-phone reception, gazing over the rolling hills and roaming herds from your private tent deck is the ultimate in high-definition viewing.

SILO'S MUSIC ROOM
530 Main St., Napa: 707-251-5833
COST: Cover charges depends on entertainment

silosnapa.com
Premier Music Room and Wine Bar features the best in live Rock, Motown, Reggae, and Jazz alongside Napa's finest wines and draft beers. Conveniently located right in Downtown Napa at the Historic Napa Mill and Napa River Inn! Open Wednesday through Saturdays.

ST. HELENA'S FARMERS' MARKET
Crane Park St., Helena: 707-486-2662
sthelenafarmersmkt.org
Fridays, 7:30 a.m. - 12 Noon; May through October. Rain or Shine. Located in Crane Park, just south of town behind the St. Helena High School.

SPAS

CALISTOGA SPA HOT SPRINGS
1006 Washington St., Calistoga: 707-942-6269
calistogaspa.com
Facilities include separate Men's and Women's Spas, four outdoor Mineral Water Pools, Exercise and Aerobics rooms, and Conference Facilities seating forty.

EURO SPA & INN
1202 Pine St., Calistoga: 707.942.6829
eurospa.com
TripAdvisor Travelers' Choice Award Winner, 2010. Relaxing & intimate atmosphere, serene pool setting, neighboring vineyard views, true hospitality, downtown Calistoga location.

GOLDEN HAVEN HOT SPRINGS
1713 Lake St., Calistoga: 707-942-8000
goldenhaven.com
Calistoga Golden Haven Hot Springs Spa is nestled in the heart of California's Napa Valley wine country and makes the perfect Calistoga spa getaway. Come and experience the magic of the Calistoga hot springs water and rejuvenating spa treatments. After a day of touring Napa Valley, you can swim in
Their hot springs pool, relax on the sun deck under the California sun, and rejuvenate with our famous Calistoga spa treatments.

LAVENDER HILL SPA
1015 Foothill Blvd., Calistoga: 707.942.4495
lavenderhillspa.com

Just a few steps from the historic Napa Valley Wine Country town of Calistoga, elegantly seated in a terraced garden hillside, you will find tiny and tranquil Lavender Hill Spa. A harmonious blend of Napa Valley Wine Country beauty with exotic Asian influenced statuary and art create the perfect setting for high quality Calistoga spa treatments.

MOUNT VIEW HOTEL & SPA
1457 Lincoln Ave., Calistoga: 707-942-6877
mountviewhotel.com

INDEX

1

111 MINNA GALLERY, 53
1300 ON FILLMORE, 41
15 ROMOLO, 47

4

440 CASTRO, 57

5

500 CLUB, 51

7

750 RESTAURANT & BAR, 23

8

83 PROOF, 53

A

ABOVE THE WINE COUNTRY BALLOONS AND TOURS, 65
ABSINTHE BRASSERIE AND BAR, 40
ACQUERELLO, 39
ADAGIO, 12
AIRPORT LODGING, 18
AKIKO'S RESTAURANT & SUSHI BAR, 26
ALAMO SQUARE SEAFOOD GRILL, 40
ALBONA RISTORANTE ISTRIANO, 45
ALCATRAZ CRUISES, 65
ALEGRIAS FOOD FROM SPAIN, 43
ALEXANDER'S STEAKHOUSE, 41
ALFRED'S STEAKHOUSE, 23
ALIOTO'S, 32

ALL ABOUT CHINATOWN WALKING TOURS, 65
ALL SEASONS BISTRO, 97
AMANTE, 47
AMBASSADOR TOYS, 78
AMBER INDIA, 26
AMERICAN, 23, 24, 25, 27, 28, 30, 33, 34, 35, 37, 41, 42, 43, 46, 95, 97, 98, 99
ANDAZ NAPA, 88
ANGELE, 94
ANTOLOGIA VINOTECA, 47
ANZU, 26
AQUARIUM OF THE BAY, 65
ARBOR GUEST HOUSE, 87
ARCHBISHOP'S MANSION, THE, 7
Asia de Cuba, 13
ASIAN, 23, 28, 34, 42
ATTIC CLUB, 51
AUB ZAM ZAM, 50
AUBERGE DU SOLEIL RESORT, 88
AUBERGE ON THE VINEYARD, 88
AUNT CHARLIE'S, 62

B

B44, 26
BABY BLUES BBQ, 34
BACCO RISTORANTE, 31
BACK ROOM WINES, 94
BADLANDS, 57
BAKER STREET BISTRO, 44
BAMBOO HUT, 49
BARBECUE, 34
BARDESSONO, 89

BAROLO, 100
BASIL CANTEEN, 42
BATH SENSE, 85
BAY AREA DISCOVERY MUSEUM, 66
BAY BRIDGE INN, 7
BAYSIDE INN AT THE WHARF, 10
BEACH BLANKET BABYLON, 66
BEACH CHALET BREWERY & RESTAURANT, 46
BEAU WINE TOURS, 66, 100
BEAZLEY HOUSE, 89
BECK'S MOTOR LODGE, 17
BENU, 42
BETTINA, 85
BIG 4 RESTAURANT, 37
Big Four, 19
BIMBO'S 365 CLUB, 47
BISOU, 31
Bistro & Bar, 88
BISTRO DON GIOVANNI, 94
BISTRO SABOR, 95
BIX, 24
BLACKBIRD, 57
BLIND CAT, 51
Bliss Spa, 17
BLOWFISH SUSHI TO DIE FOR, 34
BLUSH!, 57
BOHEME, 19
BOOKS, INC., 76
BOOTIE AT DNA LOUNGE, 53
BOSKO'S TRATTORIA, 98
BOTTLE CAP, 47
BOUDIN AT THE WHARF, 67
BOURBON STEAK, 27

BOY BAR, 57
BROWSER BOOKS, 80
BRUNO'S, 51
BULO, 82
BUTTER, 53

C

CABLE CAR MUSEUM, 73
CAFE DE LA PRESSE, 27
CAFE PESCATORE, 33
Caffe Espresso, 15
California Welcome Center San Francisco, 6
CALIFORNIAN, 24, 26, 28, 40, 41, 43
CALISTOGA FARMER'S MARKET, 101
CALISTOGA SPA HOT SPRINGS, 106
CANDLELIGHT INN, 89
CANTINA, 55
CANTON BAZAAR, 77
CAPP'S CORNER, 45
Caribbean, 32
CARNEROS INN, 90
CASA LANA B&B, 100
CASTELLO DI AMOROSA, 101
CASTRO, 31, 67
CASTRO LODGING, 17
CASTRO THEATRE, 67
CAT CLUB, 53
CEDAR GABLES INN, 90
CELADON, 95
CELLAR, THE, 55
CHADWICK'S OF LONDON, 76
CHARLES M. SCHULZ MUSEUM, 66

CHELSEA GARDEN INN, 90
CHESTNUT STREET SHOPPING, 76
CHINA STATION, 77
CHINATOWN, 68
CHINATOWN SHOPPING, 77
CHINESE, 21, 22, 23, 36
CHURCH KEY, 48
CHURCHILL, 58
CINCH, THE, 62
CIRCOLO, 52
CIVIC CENTER, 40
CLIFT, 13
Clift Hotel, 55
Club Deluxe, 50
COLIBRI MEXICAN BISTRO, 27
COMMONWEALTH, 35, 36
CONTEMPORARY JEWISH MUSEUM, 68
CONTINENTAL, 27
COOKING CLASSES IN NAPA VALLEY AREA, 100
COSMOPOLITAN, 53
COTOGNA, 24
COURTYARD BY MARRIOTT DOWNTOWN, 7
CRAB HOUSE AT PIER 39, 33
CRIB, THE, 61
CRUISIN' THE CASTRO, 67

D

DAILY GRILL, 27
DAKOTA HOTEL AND HOSTEL, 8
DAYS INN, 8
DAYS INN AT THE BEACH, 8
DECO LOUNGE, 63

DINER, 38
DIVA'S, 63
DOC'S CLOCK, 52
DOVRE CLUB, 52
DOWNTOWN LODGING, 7
DOWNTOWN/UNION SQUARE, 25
DUCK TOURS, 73

E

E&O TRADING COMPANY, 28
EDGE, 58
EDWARD DAVIS LTD., 84
EL RIO, 63
EMBARCADERO CENTER 1-4 SHOPPING, 78
EMBARCADERO/FINANCIAL DISTRICT, 23
EMPRESS OF CHINA, 21
ENDUP, 61
ENDUP, THE, 54
ESTA NOCHE, 63
EURO SPA & INN, 106
EUROPEAN, 45
EVE, 54
EZ5, 49

F

FAIRMONT HERITAGE PLACE GHIRARDELLI SQUARE, 10
FAIRMONT SAN FRANCISCO, THE, 19
FARINA, 35
Farmers' Market, 79

FERRY BUILDING MARKETPLACE, 78
FERRY PLAZA FARMERS MARKET, 68
Fifth Floor, 15
FILLMORE STREET SHOPPING, 80
FISH & FARM, 28
FISHERMAN'S WHARF, 68
FISHERMANS WHARF, 32
FLATIRON GRILL, 98
FLAX ART & DESIGN, 83
FLOUR + WATER, 35
FRAME-O-RAMA, 85
FRENCH, 27, 29, 31, 39, 40, 44, 94, 95

G

GANGWAY, 63
Garden Court, 15
GARY DANKO, 33
GHIRARDELLI SQUARE, 69
GINO & CARLO COCKTAIL LOUNGE, 48
GOLD CANE COCKTAIL LOUNGE, 50
GOLDEN GATE BRIDGE, 69
GOLDEN GATE FERRY, 70
GOLDEN GATE FORTUNE COOKIE FACTORY, 70
GOLDEN GATE HOTEL, 13
GOLDEN HAVEN HOT SPRINGS, 107
GOLDEN HAVEN HOT SPRINGS SPA AND RESORT, 90

GOURMET NAPA WALKING TOUR, 101
GRAND HYATT, 14
GRAND IMPORTS, 83
GRASSLANDS BAR & LOUNGE, 49
GRAY LINE, 70
GRIFFON, 14
GRUBSTAKE, 38

H

HAIGHT ASHBURY FLOWER POWER WALKING TOUR, 71
HAIGHT STREET SHOPPING, 80
HAIGHT-ASHBURY RESTAURANTS, 31
HALL RUTHERFORD, 102
HANG AH TEA ROOM, 22
HANGAR ONE VODKA DISTILLERY, 71
HARBOR COURT, 14
HARLOT, 54
HARRY DENTON'S STARLIGHT ROOM, 55
Harry Denton's Starlight Room, 16
HARVEY'S, 58
HAYES VALLEY SHOPPING, 81
HECHO, 24
HENNESSEY HOUSE, 91
HIDDEN VINE, THE, 49
HILTON FISHERMAN'S WHARF, 10
HOBSON'S CHOICE, 50
HOLE IN THE WALL, 61
HOLIDAY INN EXPRESS & SUITES FISHERMAN'S WHARF, 11
HOLIDAY INN FISHERMAN'S WHARF, 11
HOLY COW, 61
HOWARD JOHNSON HOTEL & SUITES, 18
HUNTINGTON, 19
HYATT AT FISHERMAN'S WHARF, 11
HYATT REGENCY SAN FRANCISCO AIRPORT, 18

I

INDIAN, 26, 30, 96
INDIAN SPRINGS, 91
INK HOUSE, THE, 91
INN ON RANDOLPH, 92
INTERCONTINENTAL MARK HOPKINS, 19
ITALIAN, 24, 25, 31, 32, 33, 35, 37, 39, 40, 45, 94, 96, 98

J

JAI YUN, 22
JAPANESE, 24, 26, 36
JOHN COLINS, 54

K

KAN ZAMAN, 32
KENWOOD INN, 92

KEZAR PUB & RESTAURANT, 50
KNIGHTS INN DOWNTOWN, 8
KOH SAMUI & THE MONKEY, 43
KOK BAR SAN FRANCISCO, 61

L

LA FOLIE, 39
LA QUINTA INN SOUTH, 18
LA TOQUE, 95
LARK CREEK STEAK, 28
LAST CALL, 58
LAVENDER, 92
LAVENDER HILL SPA, 107
LE COLONIAL, 29, 38
LEXINGTON CLUB, 63
LINCO & CO, 80
LITTLE BAOBAB, 52
LITTLE MINSKYS BURLESQUE, 50
Living Room Bar, 17
LOMBARD STREET, 71
LONE PALM, 52
LONE STAR SALOON, 62
LOOKOUT BAR, 58
LOVEJOY'S TEA ROOM, 36
LUNG SHAN CHINESE RESTAURANT, 36

M

MANDARIN ORIENTAL, 8
MARINA, 43
MARK HOPKINS, 19
MARRAKECH MAGIC THEATER, 72
MARRIOTT AT FISHERMAN'S WHARF, 11
MARRIOTT SAN FRANCISCO, 9
MARRIOTT SAN FRANCISCO AIRPORT, 18
MARS BAR & RESTAURANT, 54
MARTUNI'S, 54, 59
MAYKADEH, 45
MEADOWOOD, 93
MEXICAN, 27
MEZZANINE, 55
MICHAEL MINA, 29
Middle Eastern, 32, 45
MIDNIGHT SUN, 59
MILK BAR, 51
MILLENNIUM, 29
MINT, 59
MISSION, 34
MISSION CHINESE FOOD, 36
MISSION COMICS & ART, 84
MISSION STREET SHOPPING, 83
MIX, 59
MOBY DICK, 59
MOSSER HOTEL, THE, 9
MOUNT VIEW HOTEL & SPA, 107
MR. SMITH'S, 54
MULTIKULTI, 84
MURIO'S TROPHY ROOM, 51
MY TRICK PONY, 84

N

NAPA DOWNTOWN FARMERS' MARKET, 103
NAPA INN, THE, 93
NAPA RIVER ADVENTURES' GUIDED RIVER BOAT CRUISES, 102
NAPA VALLEY AREA SPA'S, 106
NAPA VALLEY BALLOONS, 103
NAPA VALLEY BIKE TOURS, 103
NAPA VALLEY HOTELS AND GUEST HOUSES, 87
NAPA VALLEY OPERA HOUSE, 104
Napa Valley Welcome Center, 6
NAPA VALLEY WINE TRAIN, 72
NEELA'S, 96
NEW DELHI RESTAURANT, 30
NOB HILL, 37
NOB HILL LODGING, 18
NOB HILL MOTOR INN SAN FRANCISCO, 20
Nob Hill Spa, 19
NORTH BEACH, 44, 72
NORTH BEACH SHOPPING, 82

O

OCCIDENTAL CIGAR CLUB, THE, 49
OCTAVIA'S HAZE GALLERY, 82
OENOTRI, 96
OLD VOGUE, 83
OLD WORLD INN, 93
OMNI SAN FRANCISCO HOTEL, 9
Ozumo Sushi Bar, 14

P

PACIFIC HEIGHTS, 41
PALACE, THE, 14
PALIO D'ASTI, 25
PALOMAR, 15
PAN-ASIAN, 30
PAPYRUS, 77
PEARL, 96
PERRY'S, 25
PHOENIX BAR & IRISH GATHERING HOUSE, 52
PHONE BOOTH, THE, 64
Pied Piper Bar & Grill, 15
PIER 39, 73
PILSNER INN, 59
PIPE DREAMS, 81
PIZZA, 24, 98
POLK STREET SHOPPING, 84
POSITIVELY HAIGHT STREET, 81
POWERHOUSE, 62
PUNCHLINE, THE, 49
PURE BEAUTY, 79

Q

Q BAR, 60

R

R&G LOUNGE, 22
RADISSON FISHERMAN'S WHARF, 11
RAYMOND VINEYARDS, 105
Redwood Room, 13, 55
Regency Club, 14
Remede Spa, 16
RENOIR HOTEL, 10
RESIDENCE, THE, 60
Restaurant at Meadowood, 93, 97
REX, 15
RIBBONERIE, THE, 85
RICKHOUSE, 50
RISTORANTE MILANO, 40
RITZ-CARLTON, 20
ROSEWOOD, 48
ROTUNDA AT NEIMAN MARCUS, 30
RUBY SKYE, 56
RUSSIAN HILL, 39

S

SACRAMENTO STREET SHOPPING, 85
SAFARI WEST, 105
SALUMERIA, 36
SAN FRANCISCO GIANTS, 74
San Francisco Zoo, 74
SAN REMO HOTEL, 12
Sattui, Dario, 101
SCOMA, 34
SEAFOOD, 32, 33, 38, 40, 46, 95
SEE'S CANDIES, 79
SHERATON FISHERMAN'S WHARF, 12
SHOWDOWN, THE, 55
SIKARA JEWELRY, 79
SILO'S MUSIC ROOM, 106
SIP BAR & LOUNGE, 48
SIR FRANCIS DRAKE, 15
SLIDE, 56
SMITH & HAWKEN, 80
Solage Resort, 99
SOLBAR, 99
SOMA, 41
Sonoma Valley Vintners & Growers, 6
SOUTHWESTERN, 27
Spa at Kenwood, 92
SPANISH, 26, 44, 97
ST. HELENA'S FARMERS' MARKET, 106
ST. PATRICK'S CATHOLIC CHURCH, 74
ST. REGIS, 16
STANFORD COURT, 20
Starlight Room, 16
STEAKHOUSE, 23, 26, 27, 28, 29, 38, 42, 98
STRAITS RESTAURANT, 30
STRATFORD HOTEL, 16
STRAY BAR, 64
STUD, THE, 62
SUITES AT FISHERMAN'S WHARF, 12
SUN SHADE OPTIQUE, 77
SUNSET DISTRICT, 45
SUSHI, 24, 26, 34, 36
SWAN OYSTER DEPOT, 38

T

TAPAS, 26
THAI, 42, 43
THE CULINARY INSTITUTE OF AMERICA AT GREYSTONE, 100
THE WOK SHOP, 78
THEE PARKSIDE, 64
TOAD HALL, 60
Top of the Mark, 19
TREASURE ISLAND FLEA, 83
TRIPTYCH, 43
TRUCK, 64
TSUNAMI, 37
TUNNEL TOP, 56
TWIN PEAKS, 60

U

UNDERGROUND SAN FRANCISCO, 61
UNION SQUARE, 74
UNION SQUARE HOTEL, 16
UNION SQUARE LODGING, 12
UNION SQUARE SHOPPING, 86

V

VEGA, 37
VEGAN, 29
VEGETARIAN, 29, 30, 43, 45
VER UNICA, 82
VERD'S FUNK, 81
VERDI CLUB, 52
VESSEL, 56
VESUVIO, 48
VICTORIAN HOME HISTORICAL WALKING TOUR, 75
VIETNAMESE, 29, 38
VILLAGIO, 94
VINTNER'S COLLECTIVE TASTING ROOM, 97
VITALE, 16

W

W SAN FRANCISCO, 16
WARWICK REGIS HOTEL, 17
WESTFIELD SAN FRANCISCO CENTRE, 86
WESTIN ST. FRANCIS, 17
Westin St. Francis Hotel, 29
WHARF LODGING, 10
WILD SIDE WEST, 64
WINE COUNTRY BUS TOURS, 105
WOODCHUCK ANTIQUES, 86

Y

YOSEMITE TOURS, 75
YUET LEE SEAFOOD RESTAURANT, 23

Z

ZUZU, 97

INDEX BY CUISINE

AMERICAN
750 RESTAURANT & BAR · 27
BIX · 28
PERRY'S · 29
BOURBON STEAK · 31
E&O TRADING COMPANY · 32
DAILY GRILL · 31
FISH & FARM · 32
ROTUNDA AT NEIMAN MARCUS · 34
CRAB HOUSE AT PIER 39 37
BABY BLUES BBQ · 38
COMMONWEALTH · 39, 40
BIG 4 RESTAURANT · 41
GRUBSTAKE · 42
1300 ON FILLMORE · 45
BENU · 46
TRIPTYCH · 47
BEACH CHALET BREWERY & RESTAURANT · 50
CELADON · 109
LA TOQUE · 109
ALL SEASONS BISTRO · 112
BAROLO · 112
CALISTOGA INN - 103
SOLBAR · 113

ASIAN
750 RESTAURANT & BAR · 27
E&O TRADING COMPANY · 32
BLOWFISH SUSHI TO DIE FOR · 38
ALEXANDER'S STEAKHOUSE · 45
BASIL CANTEEN · 46

BARBECUE
BABY BLUES BBQ · 38

CALIFORNIAN
BIX · 28
ANZU · 30
FISH & FARM · 32
ABSINTHE BRASSERIE AND BAR · 44
1300 ON FILLMORE · 45
TRIPTYCH · 47

CARIBBEAN
CHA CHA CHA · 32

CHINESE
EMPRESS OF CHINA · 25

HANG AH TEA ROOM · 26
JAI YUN · 26
R&G LOUNGE · 26
YUET LEE SEAFOOD RESTAURANT · 27
LUNG SHAN CHINESE RESTAURANT · 40

DINER
GRUBSTAKE · 42

EUROPEAN
ALBONA RISTORANTE ISTRIANO · 49

FRENCH
CAFE DE LA PRESSE · 31
LE COLONIAL · 32, 42
BISOU · 35
LA FOLIE · 43
ABSINTHE BRASSERIE AND BAR · 44
ALAMO SQUARE SEAFOOD GRILL · 44
BAKER STREET BISTRO · 48
ANGELE · 108
LA TOQUE · 109

INDIAN
AMBER INDIA · 30
NEW DELHI · 34
NEELA'S · 110

ITALIAN
COTOGNA · 28
PALIO D'ASTI · 29
BACCO RISTORANTE · 35
ALIOTO'S · 36
CAFE PESCATORE · 37
FARINA · 39
VEGA · 41
ACQUERELLO · 40
RISTORANTE MILANO · 44
ALBONA RISTORANTE ISTRIANO · 49
BISTRO DON GIOVANNI · 109
OENOTRI · 110
BAROLO · 100
BOSKO'S TRATTORIA · 112

JAPANESE
HECHO · 28
AKIKO'S RESTAURANT & SUSHI BAR · 29
TSUNAMI · 40

MEXICAN
COLIBRI MEXICAN BISTRO · 31

MIDDLE EASTERN
KAN ZAMAN · 36
MAYKADEH · 49

PAN-ASIAN
STRAITS RESTAURANT · 34

PIZZA
COTOGNA · 28
BOSKO'S TRATTORIA · 112

SEAFOOD
ALIOTO'S · 36
CAFE PESCATORE · 37
CRAB HOUSE AT PIER 39 · 37
SWAN OYSTER DEPOT · 42
RISTORANTE MILANO · 44
BEACH CHALET BREWERY & RESTAURANT · 50
CELADON · 109

SOUTHWESTERN
COLIBRI MEXICAN BISTRO · 31

STEAKHOUSE
ALFRED'S STEAKHOUSE · 27
BOURBON STEAK · 31
ANZU · 30
DAILY GRILL · 31
LARK CREEK STEAK · 32
HOUSE OF PRIME RIB · 39
ALEXANDER'S STEAKHOUSE · 45
FLATIRON GRILL · 113

SPANISH
B44 · 30
ALEGRIAS FOOD FROM SPAIN · 47
ZUZU · 111

SUSHI
HECHO · 28
AKIKO'S RESTAURANT & SUSHI BAR · 29
ANZU · 30
BLOWFISH SUSHI TO DIE FOR · 38
TSUNAMI · 37

TAPAS
B44 · 30

THAI
BASIL CANTEEN · 46

VEGAN
MILLENNIUM · 33

VEGETARIAN
MILLENNIUM · 33
NEW DELHI · 34
KOH SAMUI & THE MONKEY · 47
MAYKADEH · 49

VIETNAMESE
Le Colonial – 30

Other Books by the Same Author

Available in quality bookstores as well all online retailers.

JACK HOUSTON ST. CLAIR SERIES

THE KEYSTONE FILE – PART 1 – A Jack Houston St. Clair Political Thriller
Florida Governor Sam Houston St. Clair is the Republican candidate for President. On Election Night it's discovered that there's been a tie in the Electoral College, resulting in a deadlock. The Constitution requires that in such a case the election is thrown into the House of Representatives, where each state has a single vote. Incumbent Republican President Jeffrey Norwalk is determined that St. Clair will succeed him because he expects St. Clair to continue his policies and he plans to use the secret Keystone File to achieve his agenda. [Prequel to **The Running Mate.** Action takes place four years earlier.]

THE KEYSTONE FILE – PART 2 – A Jack Houston St. Clair Political Thriller
President Norwalk has convened a special session of Congress for the ostensible purpose of preparing to elect his replacement. The real reason, however, is so his congressional liaison deputy, Phil Slanetti, can go to work on individual members.

Governor St. Clair and everybody else in the American political establishment descend on Washington to begin the arm-twisting. Son Jack and girlfriend Babylon (Babe) Fuentes lend a hand by moving to Washington as well.

Back in Miami, Babe's mother Ramona is dealing with a persistent Derek Gilbertson (her daughter Raven's ex-husband, who is still a member of her prestigious law firm) who is pushing her to approve some shady financial transactions. Ramona hires Jack's agency to tail Derek. Meanwhile, Jack's brother, Lieutenant Rafael St. Clair, takes a DEA undercover agent who had been adrift in a Zodiac aboard his Coast Guard cutter *Fearless* in the Florida straights. [Prequel to **The Running Mate.** Action takes place four years earlier.]

THE KEYSTONE FILE – PART 3 – A Jack Houston St. Clair Political Thriller

While Jack tries to help his dad swing the election in the House of Representatives, he also gets involved in following Derek Gilbertson, partner in Ramona Fuentes's law firm. Derek married Ramona's daughter, Raven, who was Jack's ex-lover. Now Jack's sleeping with Babylon Fuentes, Raven's younger sister

We also discover that Jack's younger brother, Rafael St. Clair, is having an affair with the other Fuentes daughter,

Antonia, further complicating the St. Clair and Fuentes families.

While Phil Slanetti works his way through the House membership with the Keystone File, Wyoming Congressman-elect Matt Hawkins falls in love with Patrician Vaughan, whose gay husband could care less about her.

When Ramon asks Jack to tail Derek because she has suspicions about his international banking activity he runs through the law firm, Jack gets involved in more than he planned on.

And when President Norwalk takes Sam Houston St. Clair to Camp David tow grill a couple of steaks and to tell him about the Keystone File, Sam realizes *how* he will get elected to the Presidency if it all works out the way Norwalk has planned. [Part 3 of the Prequel to **The Running Mate.** Action takes place four years earlier.]

THE RUNNING MATE - A Jack Houston St. Clair Political Thriller

Sam Houston St. Clair has been President for four long years and right now he's bogged down in a nasty fight to be re-elected. A Secret Service agent protecting the opposing candidate discovers that the candidate is sleeping with someone he shouldn't be, and tells his lifelong friend, the President's son Jack, this vital information so Jack can pass it on to help his father win the election.

The candidate's wife has also found out about the clandestine affair and plots to kill the lover if her husband wins the election.
Jack goes to Washington, and becomes involved in an international whirlpool of intrigue.

MARY FREEMAN SERIES

MIDNIGHT MASS - *A Mary Freeman Thriller*

Det. Lt. Mary Freeman stumbles upon a spectacular robbery of historic Trinity Church in downtown Manhattan on Christmas Eve, and after impressing the Mayor, gets assigned to the Task Force investigating the crime, throwing her headlong into a world of political intrigue and murder that rips apart every aspect of her life.

JAKE BRICKER SERIES

THE METER MAID MURDERS - *A Jake Bricker Comic Thriller*

A serial killer is loose on South Beach. But he's only killing meter maids, threatening the economic foundation of Miami Beach. Mayor Johnny Germane wants the killer caught NOW! But tall, dark and handsome Det. Sgt. Jake Bricker can't seem to nab the devious killer, even though he knows who the next victim will be. [Foul language; not for kids.]

THE ADVENTURES OF SHERLOCK HOLMES IV

In this series, the original Sherlock Holmes's great-great-great grandson solves crimes and mysteries in the present day, working out of the boutique hotel he owns on South Beach.

THE BORNHOLM DIAMOND

A mysterious Swedish nobleman requests a meeting to discuss a matter of such serious importance that it may threaten the line of succession in one of the oldest royal houses in Europe.

THE RED-HAIRED MAN

A man with a shock of red hair calls on Sherlock Holmes to solve the mystery of the Red-haired League.

THE CLEVER ONE

A former nun who, while still very devout, has renounced her vows so that she could "find a life, and possibly love, in the real world." She comes to Holmes in hopes that he can find out what happened to the man who promised to marry her, but mysteriously disappeared moments before their wedding.

THE COPPER BEECHES

A nanny reaches out to Sherlock Holmes seeking his advice on whether she should take a new position when her prospective employer has demanded that she cut her hair as part of the job.

THE MAN WITH THE TWISTED LIP

In what seems to be the case of a missing person, Sherlock Holmes navigates his way through a maze of perplexing clues that leads him through a sinister world to a surprising conclusion

THE DEVIL'S FOOT

Holmes's doctor orders him to take a short holiday in Key West, and while there, Holmes is called on to look into a case in which three people involved in a Santería ritual died with no explanation.

THE BOSCOMBE VALLEY MYSTERY

Sherlock Holmes and Watson are called to a remote area of Florida overlooking Lake Okeechobee to investigate a murder where all the evidence points to the victim's son as the killer. Holmes, however, is not so sure.

THE SIX NAPOLEONS

Inspector Lestrade calls on Holmes to help him figure out why a madman would go around Miami breaking into homes and businesses to destroy cheap busts of the French Emperor. It all seems very insignificant to Holmes—until, of course, a murder occurs.

THE TRAP DOOR SERIES

THE TRAP DOOR: THE "LOST" SCRIPT OF *CARDENIO*

A boy goes back to 1594 and Shakespeare's original Globe Theatre in search of a "lost" play by the world's greatest writer, and ends up embroiled in the plot to kill Queen Elizabeth the First and replace her with Mary, Queen of

Scots. [Highly suitable for kids.]

THE ANNALS OF SANTOPIA

SANTOPIA: PART I, BOOK 1 – SANTA & THE LOST PRINCESS

Three days before Christmas in the year 1900, Connie Claus has a son, and Santa names the boy Nicholas. Ameritus, Great Sage of Santopia, issues a Prophecy – the next girl born in the Kingdom will grow up to become Prince Nicky's Queen, and Nicky will become betrothed to her on his eighteenth birthday when he is invested as the future Santa at the Ritual of the Green Gloves. Far across Frozen Lake, the Baroness von Drear gives birth to a baby girl – she's overjoyed that her new baby will be the future Queen of Santopia. But when she discovers another girl was born just hours before her own to Taraxa and Inula, peasant family living in her Realm, she sets out to destroy them.

SANTOPIA: PART I, BOOK 2: SANTA & THE TRUTH REVEALED

It's Christmas Eve, and Elf Duncan journeys to the Other World as a stowaway on the Grand Sleigh. When discovered, he is forced to stay with the Red Elves in their Warren deep below the Tower of London until Santa can send a sleigh to bring him home. Back in Santopia during the same time period, Spicata rescues Taraxa and Inula from the carnivorous Pirandelves and gets them safely to Santopolis where he hopes to discover the *real* story behind the missing baby girl, thinking his reward would be great if he could get new information to the Baroness.

SCREENPLAYS

MIDNIGHT MASS – THE SCREENPLAY

Det. Lt. Mary Freeman stumbles upon a spectacular robbery of historic Trinity Church in downtown Manhattan on Christmas Eve, and after impressing the Mayor, gets assigned to the Task Force investigating the crime, throwing her headlong into a world of political intrigue and murder that rips apart every aspect of her life. (Based on the novel.)

MEETING SPENCER – THE SCREENPLAY

After a series of Hollywood flops, famed director Harris Chappell (Jeffrey Tambor in the movie released in 2012) returns to New York to relaunch his Broadway career. But Chappell's triumphant comeback begins to spiral out of control into a wild night of comic misadventure after meeting struggling actor Spencer (Jesse Plemons) and his old flame Didi (Melinda McGraw). This is an original script (not based on a novel or other source material). This is the original script, NOT the shooting script. You can stream the movie on Netflix. Or buy it on Amazon.

THE TRAP DOOR – THE SCREENPLAY

Looking for a famous "lost" play, a London boy performing in "A Midsummer Night's Dream" travels back in time to 1594 and the original production of the play in the original Globe Theatre. While there, he becomes embroiled in a plot to assassinate the Protestant Queen Elizabeth the First and replace her with the Catholic Mary, Queen of Scots. (Based on the novel.)

DELAPLAINE TRAVEL GUIDES

Delaplaine Travel Guides represent the author's take on some of the many cities he's visited and many of which he has called hom

These books are updated 3 times per year, both in print and in Ebook form.

Current editions available:

Delaplaine's 2013 Guide to South Beach

Delaplaine's 2013 Guide to Miami & South Beach

Delaplaine's 2013 Guide to Key West & the Florida Keys

Delaplaine's 2013 Guide to Fort Lauderdale

Delaplaine's 2013 Guide to Las Vegas

Delaplaine's 2013 Guide to Orlando & Walt Disney World

Delaplaine's 2013 Guide to San Francisco